Dorset
from the Air

Claire Pinder, Steve Wallis and Laurence Keen

DORSET BOOKS

In association with the National Monuments Record

NATIONAL
MONUMENTS
RECORD

First published in 1998 by Dorset Books
© 1998 Dorset County Council

Photographs Copyright
5, 13a, 16, 17, 19, 20, 25, 30, 34, 35, 36, 37, 41, 45, 47, 50, 53, 59, 61, 63, 64, 65, 68, 69, 70, 73, 76, 79, 80, 90, 92, 93, 94, 95, 119, 121, 122, 123, 124, 139, 140 Francesca Radcliffe; 4, 7, 8, 23, 26, 27, 28, 32, 38, 42, 48, 51, 55, 58, 71, 77, 78, 81, 82, 83, 86, 87, 97, 102, 108, 115, 125, 128, 131, 132, 133, 134, 135, 136, 138 Crown Copyright RCHME; 1, 2, 3, 6, 11, 12, 13, 14, 15, 18, 21, 22, 24, 29, 33, 39, 40, 43, 44, 46, 49, 52, 54, 56, 57, 60, 62, 66, 67, 72, 74, 75, 84, 85, 88, 89, 91, 96, 98, 99, 103, 104, 105, 106, 107, 109, 111, 112, 113, 114, 116, 117, 118, 126, 127, 129, 130, 133, 137 Dorset County Council; 100, 101, 110 The Ministry of Defence/RAF; 120 Devon County Council; 136, 138 John Boyden; 31 R.N.R. Peers.

ISBN 1 87116 445 1

British Library Cataloguing-in-Publication-Data
A CIP data for this book is available from the British Library

DORSET BOOKS
Halsgrove House
Lower Moor Way
Tiverton EX16 6SS
T: 01884 243242
F: 01884 243325
www.halsgrove.com

Printed and bound in England by WBC Ltd, Bridgend

Contents

Archaeological Periods

Note: the dates given are approximate.

Palaeolithic (to 10,000 BC)
Mobile, hunter-gatherer groups in tundra-like landscape. Around 10,000 BC climate warming brings about vegetational change to predominant pine/birch woodland, with consequent improvements in soil quality and available food resources.

Mesolithic (10,000 BC to 3500 BC)
Changes in worked flint tools reflect changes to the hunting of woodland animals. Typical occupation sites are coastal, to take advantage of marine resources, and upland, to exploit herds grazing the more open areas. Towards the end of the Mesolithic period there are attempts to modify or control the environment. For example, in some areas evidence of forest burning and limited clearance has been identified.

Neolithic (3500 BC to 2000 BC)
The Neolithic saw the adoption of farming as the basis of a subsistence economy. Settlements become more permanent, there is increasing use of pottery and the introduction of quern stones for the grinding of corn. Causewayed enclosures are built, and a culture develops in which burial grounds are elaborated by the construction of monumental mounds and cairns. Other ceremonial features such as cursus are constructed.

Bronze Age (2,000 BC to 650 BC)
The growth of metalworking from around 2000 BC seems at first to have been used to produce luxury items and had little effect on farming. Burial mounds take the form of round barrows, often clustered around earlier monuments. In the later Bronze Age some settlements were enclosed behind pallisades, others were abandoned, and this seems to have been a decline of arable farming in favour of cattle.

Iron Age (650 BC to AD 43)
Hill-forts are constructed. Iron working technology develops and becomes widely available. Iron can be used to make basic farming equipment and tools. Coastal areas develop strong trading links with the continent. Towards the end of the Iron Age, the Roman Empire begins to exert a powerful influence on the economy and culture of south-eastern England in particular. The Iron Age ends with the Roman invasion in AD 43. Following the military occupation, a Roman style of administration and taxation is imposed. Despite this, life in many rural areas seems to have continued virtually unchanged.

Foreword

This book is based on an exhibition, also called *Dorset from the Air*, which was held at the Dorset Record Office in Dorchester between March and August 1996. The exhibition was visited by over 350 people and formed the setting for a successful dayschool, organised by the Dorset County Council Archaeological Service, on the uses of aerial photography in archaeology. Such was the interest expressed by visitors to the exhibition that a decision was taken to publish the material. This book would not have been possible without the work of photographers Francesca Radcliffe (and her pilot Giles Romanes) and Steve Wallis.

Particular thanks are due to: Anna Eavis and Sharon Soutar (National Monuments Record); David Wilson (Cambridge University Committee for Aerial Photography); Frances Griffith (Devon County Council); David Belson (Crown Copyright Administrator, Ministry of Defence); Steve Spring, Mark Simons and George Hussey (Dorset County Council); John Boyden and Francesca Radcliffe for assistance of various kinds rendered during the process of photograph selection and preparation of artwork. In addition, Nigel Tyndall, Barbara Pinder and Francesca Radcliffe undertook the awful task of reading and commenting on the draft text.

Photographs are reproduced by kind permission of the following:

Francesca Radcliffe (**FR**), The National Monuments Record of the Royal Commission on the Historical Monuments of England, Dorset County Council (**DCC** and **SW** – Steve Wallis, Dorset County Council Archaeology Service), Devon County Council, The Ministry of Defence (RAF), John Boyden, and R.N.R. Peers.

A high-winged Cessna aircraft. Manoevreable, and with wings in a position which does not obscure the view, this aircraft is of a type ideal for oblique aerial photography.

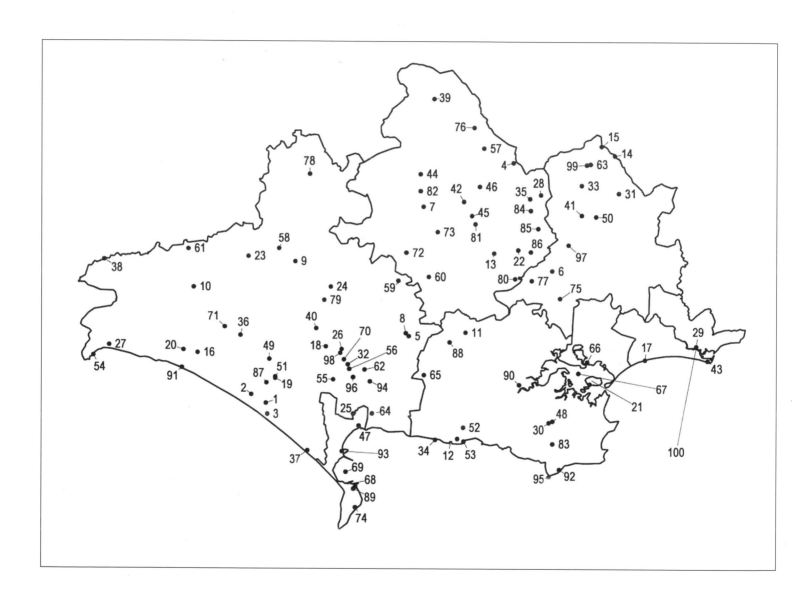

Map and List of Places Mentioned

1 Abbotsbury
2 Abbotsbury Castle
3 Abbotsbury Swannery
4 Ashmore
5 Athelhampton
6 Badbury Rings
7 Banbury Hill, Okeford Fitzpaine
8 Bardolfeston, Puddletown
9 Batcombe
10 Beaminster
11 Bere Regis
12 Bindon Hill
13 Blandford Forum
14 Bokerley Dyke
15 Bokerley Junction
16 Bothenhampton
17 Bournemouth
18 Bradford Peverell
19 Bridehead, Littlebredy
20 Bridport
21 Brownsea Island
22 Buzbury Rings, Tarrant Keyneston
23 Castle Hill, Chelborough
24 Cerne Abbas
25 Chalbury, Bincombe

26 Charminster
27 Charmouth
28 Chettle
29 Christchurch
30 Corfe Castle
31 Cranborne
32 Dorchester
33 the Dorset Cursus
34 Durdle Door
35 Eastbury, Tarrant Gunville
36 Eggardon
37 the Fleet
38 Forde Abbey, Thorncombe
39 Gillingham
40 Grimston Down
41 Gussage All Saints
42 Hambledon Hill
43 Hengistbury Head
44 Hinton St Mary
45 Hod Hill, Stourpaine
46 Iwerne Minster
47 Jordan Hill
48 Kingston Down, Corfe Castle
49 Kingston Russell Stone Circle
50 Knowlton, Woodlands

51 Littlebredy
52 Lulworth Castle
53 Lulworth Cove
54 Lyme Regis
55 Maiden Castle
56 Maumbury Rings
57 Melbury Beacon
58 Melbury Bubb
59 Melcombe Horsey
60 Milton Abbey
61 Mohun Castle, South Perrott
62 Mount Pleasant, West Stafford
63 Oakley Down
64 Osmington White Horse
65 Piddle Valley
66 Poole
67 Poole Harbour
68 Portland Castle
69 Portland Harbour
70 Poundbury
71 Powerstock Castle
72 Rawlesbury Camp, Stoke Wake
73 Ringmoor
74 Rufus Castle
75 St Aldhelm's Chapel

76 Shaftesbury
77 Shapwick
78 Sherborne
79 Smacam Down
80 Spetisbury Rings
81 Stourpaine
82 Sturminster Newton
83 Swanworth Quarry
84 Tarrant Hinton
85 Tarrant Monkton
86 Tarrant Rushton
87 Tenant's Hill, Kingston Russell
88 Throop
89 the Verne, Portland
90 Wareham
91 West Bay, Bridport
92 West Man, Worth Matravers
93 Weymouth
94 Whitcombe
95 Wimborne Minster
96 Winterborne Farringdon
97 Witchampton
98 Wolfeton House, Charminster
99 Wor Barrow
100 Wyke Down, Gussage All Saints

7

1. Hod Hill, Stourpaine
(SW, 21 July 1995)

Introduction to Aerial Photography

Archaeologists use aerial photographs in a number of ways. Large areas can be surveyed relatively easily and cheaply, and it is possible both to look for new archaeological features and to study known sites. Even features which survive as earthworks can be difficult to understand from the ground, particularly if they cover large areas, and often it is possible to get a better understanding of a monument by looking at an aerial photograph.

1. Hod Hill is the largest Iron Age hill-fort in Dorset; the multiple ramparts enclose nearly 22 hectares. It survives in good condition as a massive earthwork and has been excavated extensively. Nevertheless, a photograph such as this can give much information about the site.

The hill-fort occupies high ground in a commanding position which the invading Romans clearly appreciated, since one corner of the hill-fort on the highest part of the hill was reused as a Roman fort (see photograph **2**). The typical 'playing-card' shape was slightly modified to fit into the ramparts, but the internal layout followed the usual plan of Roman forts, with administrative buildings towards the centre and barracks at the edges. Parts of these internal buildings are reputed to have been still standing in 1858, when much of the interior of the hill-fort was ploughed. The south-eastern corner was not ploughed, and here the remains of pits and hut circles can be seen more clearly (**3**).

2. Close-up of the Roman fort on Hod Hill (SW, 13 July 1994)

3. *Close-up of hut circles in the unploughed corner of Hod Hill (SW, 13 July 1994)*

9

4. Gussage All Saints
(National Monuments Record,
8 May 1980)

Aerial photographs play an even more important part in helping us to identify and understand archaeological sites which no longer survive as earthworks.

4. Gussage All Saints. This huge oval feature might show up at ground level as a change in soil colour or perhaps as slight differences in crop growth, but we would have little idea of the nature or extent of this site without an aerial photograph. As it is, though we can say that there is what appears to be a prehistoric enclosure in this field, we have little idea of its function or date.

5. Crop-marks of enclosures, Powerstock
(FR, 8 May 1995)

5. A cluster of square enclosures show up as darker lines in a parched field near the village of Powerstock. The grass in the darker areas still shows green, suggesting that these features are ditches. Some of the darker spots in the field may be pits. The form of these enclosures suggests that they are prehistoric, perhaps an Iron Age or Romano-British farmstead, but this cannot be confirmed without more archaeological information.

6. Parch-marks of a prehistoric enclosure, Tarrant Hinton
(SW, 20 July 1994)

6. Tarrant Hinton. An enclosure revealed by parch-marks in grass. This enclosure, first identified on an aerial photograph over fifty years ago, has been recorded in different guises on many photographs over the years. The shape of the enclosure and its association with surrounding field systems suggest that it is of Iron Age or Romano-British date.

Early photographs

Two relatively early vertical photographs of earthworks.

7. West Man, Worth Matravers
(National Monuments Record, 26 October 1926)

8. Kingston Down, Corfe Castle
(National Monuments Record, 10 February 1928)

7. West Man, Worth Matravers. Massive strip lynchets are the remains of the medieval open field system around the village. These earthworks are almost as well preserved and extensive today as they were when this photograph was taken. Winspit is at the right-hand edge of the picture.

8. Kingston Down, Corfe Castle. An extensive prehistoric field-system covers many acres in the southern part of Corfe Castle parish. A double boundary which runs diagonally across the photograph and broadens out (towards the bottom left) into a 'funnel' is probably a trackway. It is generally thought that such funnel-like features were used in the management and movement of stock around the field system. Here and there the regularly-shaped fields are interrupted by roughly circular enclosures which are thought to be areas of settlement. Surface finds suggest an Iron Age/Romano-British date.

The earliest aerial photographs of archaeological sites were taken from air balloons, and the first known aerial photographs of a British archaeological site was of Stonehenge, taken from a balloon by Lt. Sharpe in 1906. The manufacture of more sophisticated aircraft and the realisation, during World War I, that aerial photography could be used for gathering military intelligence, led to the development of skills which were later put to use for archaeological purposes.

The first Archaeological Officer of the Ordnance Survey, O.G.S. Crawford, realised the potential of aerial photography as a method for recognising archaeological features. In the early 1920s, with the assistance of Alexander Keiller, Crawford carried out a photographic study of sites in Wessex, which was subsequently published in 1928 as *Wessex from the Air*. The sites in *Wessex from the Air* are mostly earthworks, and the photographs were taken with a vertical camera mounted on the aircraft. A number of well-known Dorset sites appear in the book, including Hod Hill and Badbury Rings. Early photographs were taken using glass negatives which, when they survive, give prints of remarkable clarity.

More pioneering work was carried out by Professor St Joseph of Cambridge University. The Cambridge University Committee for Aerial Photography still undertakes aerial reconnaissance and maintains a large collection of photographs.

Vertical aerial photographs

There are two main types of aerial photograph: vertical and oblique.

Vertical aerial photographs can be taken as single shots, but are generally taken from an aeroplane which has been specially adapted to allow a series of overlapping photographs to be taken from a camera which is pointing directly at the ground. This type of photograph is usually taken over large areas by military or specialist commercial aerial photographers, and for non-archaeological purposes. One of the major uses of vertical photography is mapping, though nowadays the photographs used tend to be images taken from satellites rather than aeroplanes.

Vertical photographs, unlike oblique photos, give blanket coverage of large areas. There is no selection of sites to be photographed, so examination of vertical aerial photographs is particularly useful when looking for previously-unrecognised sites. If pairs of overlapping vertical aerial photographs are viewed using a stereoscope a three-dimensional effect is created; an optical illusion throws upstanding features such as trees, buildings and earthworks into an exaggerated relief. There is quite an overlap between vertical photographs: one point on the ground usually appears on three consecutive prints.

Despite their resemblance to maps, vertical photographs do not record features exactly to scale. Though it is possible to produce useful maps by sketch-plotting archaeological features from vertical photographs, a considerable trigonometric effort is required before highly accurate plotting can be achieved.

The earliest widely available vertical photographs were taken by the RAF in the late 1940s as part of a national survey. The blanket coverage of the country provided by this set of photographs provides an important baseline of information against which later photographs can be compared.

The photograph of the Piddle Valley (**9**) was taken as part of that survey. Traces of prehistoric field-systems cover many miles of the Dorset landscape, but in only a very few places do the field boundaries survive as earthworks. It is more usual to see them as soil-marks after ploughing, as in this photograph, where the chalky field banks appear as lighter marks in the plough soil.

Local authorities continue to commission sets of vertical aerial photographs. Photograph **10** is part of a survey of the whole county acquired by Dorset County Council in 1972, and shows the area around Chettle House in North Dorset. Chettle was built around 1700, probably by Thomas Archer, for George Chafin MP. Note the soil-marks of prehistoric 'banjo' enclosures and field systems towards the bottom left of this photograph.

Increasingly aerial surveys of particular areas are commissioned by companies and individuals to facilitate survey and development projects. Some of these sets of photographs have been deposited in publicly-accessible archives (for example, a colour survey of the south-eastern part of Dorset commissioned by AMOCO in 1992 and subsequently donated to Dorset County Council).

9. The Piddle Valley

10. Chettle House

The vertical photographs on the following pages are part of a survey taken for Dorset County Council in 1997.

11. Blandford Forum lies on the River Stour, the junction of several important roads at a point where there was once a ford and is now a bridge over the river. The name Blandford is thought to come from the Old English for 'ford where blay (or gudgeon) are found'. A relatively late development, Blandford was a simple manor at the time of the Domesday Survey in 1086. Records show that there was a market here in 1217–18, and Blandford quickly became a borough and market town of some consequence. The importance of the market is reflected in the town's later medieval names of Cheping Blandford and Blandford Forum; both additions are references to the market and the latter, of course, remains in use today.

Something of the layout of the medieval town can be seen in the present street pattern, with two main roads converging on the river (towards the bottom of this photograph). Elsewhere, there are hints of a grid layout in the street pattern, suggesting an episode of deliberate town planning at some point, probably in the thirteenth century. In June 1731 over three quarters of the town was destroyed by fire. The Blandford Corporation petitioned Parliament for an Act 'for the Better and more Easy Rebuilding' of Blandford Forum, and the Act was duly passed in 1732. One important clause in the Act stipulated that non-flammable roofing materials should be used on any new buildings. Local builder-architects, brothers John and William Bastard, played an important part in the creation of the new town centre, which survives virtually intact to this day. The medieval street pattern was retained, with the enlargement of the marketplace being the only significant change.

12. Sturminster Newton. A prominent feature, to the south of the present town and at the bottom of this photograph, is Sturminster Newton 'Castle', a natural promontory on which has been constructed an Iron Age fort. A medieval manor house which for a long time belonged to Glastonbury Abbey stood inside the castle, though the present ruins here are fourteenth century. The early history of the town is uncertain, but there is some documentary evidence to suggest that it developed from settlement around two centres: the abbey manor to the south, and an early church to the north. King Alfred bequeathed an estate at *Sturemynster* to his son Aethelweard. This is generally thought to have been Sturminster, and suggests that there was a minster church here by the late ninth century. This early church may have occupied the same site as the present parish church. The cloth and leather industries seem to have been important to the economy of the medieval town. Fiddleford Mill, to the east of the town, seems to have been the site of a fulling mill in the fourteenth century. The present mill is fourteenth century with sixteenth-century additions.

*11. Blandford Forum
(DCC, August 1997)*

12. Sturminster Newton
(DCC, July 1997)

13. Beaminster
(DCC, September 1997)

13a. (inset) The parish church
of St Mary, Beaminster
(FR, 23 March 1997)

14. Gillingham
(SW, 13 July 1994)

15. (inset) King's Court
Palace
(SW, 15 January 1994)

13. Beaminster is a small market town at the confluence of several streams. An early Old English form of the name is *Bebyngmynster*, thought to mean 'the minster or church of Bebbe or her people'. Early documents suggest that there may have been a religious establishment, perhaps a nunnery founded by Bebbe or Bega, here in the ninth century, though no trace of it remains. Beaminster later passed into the manor of the bishop of Sherborne, and Bishop Wulfsige died while visiting Beaminster in 1002. Eighty-two inhabitants and three mills were recorded in the Domesday Survey.

The streams on which the town stands and Fuller's Earth clay, abundant in the area, seem to have been the foundation of the development of Beaminster as a minor industrial and trading centre in the course of the medieval period. Woollen cloth was pounded in a mixture of Fuller's Earth and water to remove natural oils, thus thickening the fabric and preparing it to take a dye. At first this was done by treading the fabric in wooden troughs, but quickly became mechanised. Primitive mills driven by water-wheels were established as early as the thirteenth century. In 1332 the Lay Subsidy Roll records names such as *Degher*, *Tailor*, *Glover*, *Choluner* (*chalon* = a worsted cloth), *Tanner*, and *Couller*.

By the fifteenth century the town seems to have been comparable in size to Blandford or Wareham. A population of about 1700 was recorded in 1775. By this time Beaminster was a local centre for both paper and cloth making. A number of disastrous fires in the seventeenth and eighteenth centuries destroyed much of the medieval town, and most of the buildings in the present town centre are the result of rebuilding in the eighteenth century, though the streets follow the medieval layout . The inset photograph shows the parish church of St Mary, probably on the site of the early church, with the triangular marketplace at the top of the photograph.

14. Gillingham. There is considerable evidence of Romano-British settlement around the modern town. The name Gillingham is thought to mean place of shelter on a road, and is often found near Roman roads or occupation sites. No direct archaeological evidence has been found to show that the presence of the Roman settlement influenced the later development of a town in this location.

Gillingham was first recorded in 1016, and had strong royal links in the early medieval period. Documents show that William Rufus and Henry I spent time at Gillingham, and King John had a hunting lodge built here in his royal forest of Gillingham. The earthwork of King's Court Palace (at the right-hand edge of photograph **14** and inset **15**), south-east of the town, is thought to be the site of this lodge. The lodge had fallen out of use by around 1300, and was sold for materials in 1369. The surrounding park remained in use until the late fifteenth century.

The town's present street pattern follows the medieval one, with four roads converging on the church. The medieval parish church was largely rebuilt in 1838, and it seems probable that any pre-Conquest church stood on the same site, particularly as part of a ninth-century cross has been found in the vicinity. South of the church is a triangular area which was the site of a medieval market, now infilled. There may have been another market, also now partly infilled, to the north east. No early buildings survive, owing to a series of fires, and the present town is built in locally made brick. A silk mill was established in Gillingham around 1769, the beginning of an important local industry.

16. Melcombe Horsey
(FR, 6 January 1995)

Oblique aerial photographs

Oblique aerial photographs are usually taken with a hand-held camera from an ordinary aeroplane. Unlike vertical photographs, oblique photographs do not give blanket coverage of an area, since the photographer selects the site to be photographed. Oblique photographs are taken specifically for archaeological purposes. Archaeologists working for the Royal Commission on the Historical Monuments of England have taken, and continue to take, many oblique photographs of archaeological features. The RCHME curates and makes available to the public a vast archive of both oblique and vertical aerial photographs at the National Monuments Record Centre in Swindon. The efforts of a large number of amateur photographers have over the years contributed greatly to aerial photographic archives. Locally, the work of John Boyden and Francesca Radcliffe (photographers) and Giles Romanes (pilot) has been of particular importance in improving our understanding of Dorset's archaeology. In recent years Steve Wallis of the Dorset County Council Archaeology Service has taken a number of oblique photographs of archaeological features.

16. Melcombe Horsey. An oblique photograph of medieval settlement remains in the park of Bingham's Melcombe House. Seen from the south, the settlement is divided by a hollow way running west–east. St Andrew's church is of fourteenth- and fifteenth-century date, but was much repaired in 1844. The present house is largely seventeenth century with eighteenth-century additions and alterations, but incorporates a fifteenth-century gatehouse, and was restored in 1893–4. The gardens retain elements of a sixteenth-century garden scheme.

17. Tenants Hill, Kingston Russell. An enclosure surrounded by a bank and ditch with what appears to be an entrance on the eastern side (on the right of this photograph). Even the long shadows thrown by a low light in this near-vertical photograph do not make visible any features in the interior of the enclosure, though the surrounding field system suggests that it is a small prehistoric settlement or stock enclosure.

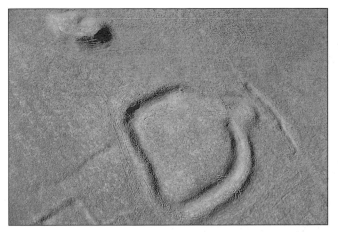

17. Tenants Hill, Kingston Russell
(FR, 4 February 1995)

18. Banbury Hill, Okeford Fitzpaine
(SW, 20 July 1994)

18. Banbury Hill-fort, Okeford Fitzpaine. Though it survives as an earthwork, this simple multi-vallate hill-fort is difficult to appreciate from the ground. An oblique photograph enables us to see its modest defences more clearly.

23

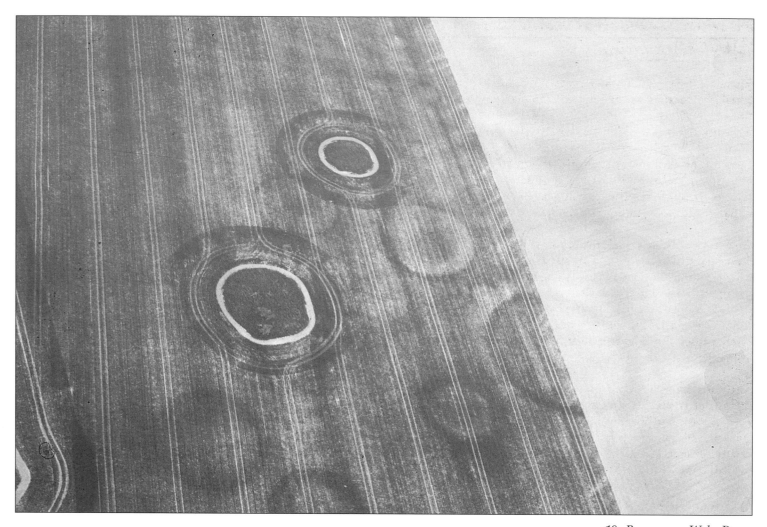

19. Barrows on Wyke Down
(FR, 28 April 1991)

19. Barrows on Wyke Down, Gussage All Saints. This photograph reveals earthworks and crop-marks in the field on the left and soil-marks in the chalky ploughed field on the right.

How archaeological features show up on aerial photographs

There are three ways in which archaeological features show up on aerial photographs: as shadows, as crop-marks, or as soil-marks.

Shadows. Features which stand up in relief will throw shadows in the right conditions. The best results are achieved at those times of the day and year when the sun is low. Such features are usually earthworks, but the growth of vegetation may be affected by underlying archaeological features, and this differential growth too can throw shadows.

Soil-marks. After ploughing sites may show up as different coloured patches in the soil as archaeological material is dragged to the surface by the plough. Colour is important in the interpretation of such soil-marks. For example, soil containing lots of organic material, perhaps the filling of a ditch or pit, tends to be dark. The movement of the plough across the field often causes the edges of features to have a curious zigzag appearance as material is dragged in different directions.

Crop-marks. Underlying archaeological features can affect the growth of crops. Hard features such as walls tend to restrict root growth and the availability of water. Plants make poor growth and are more susceptible to drought. Soft, moisture-retaining features like ditches tend to promote strong, early growth and plants will be less quickly affected by drought. The precise effect depends on the crop and its state of maturity, on the background moisture content of the soil, and may vary through the season. It is very difficult to predict when crop-marks will appear, and they may appear for only a few days, or even hours, as soil conditions change and as the crop ripens. In some circumstances, usually after long periods of drought, parch-marks may appear. Parch-marks appear most often in grass or grass-type crops and are caused in much the same way as crop-marks.

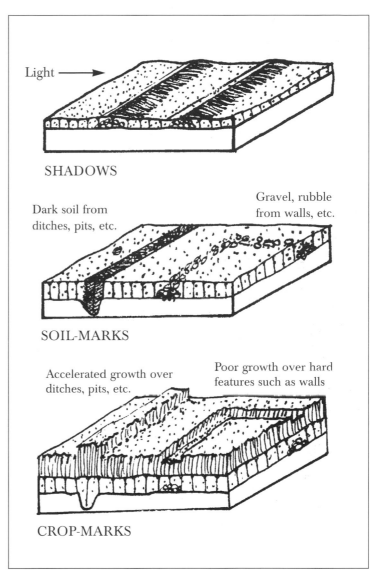

SHADOWS

SOIL-MARKS

Dark soil from ditches, pits, etc.

Gravel, rubble from walls, etc.

CROP-MARKS

Accelerated growth over ditches, pits, etc.

Poor growth over hard features such as walls

Light →

Diagram after Darvill (1987)

20. Bardolfeston, Puddletown
(FR, 17 August 1994)

(Below) Plan of Bardolfeston,
after Platt (1978)

20. Bardolfeston, Puddletown. The earthworks of this deserted medieval village are enhanced by a low winter light. House platforms and the rectangular enclosures in which they stand are visible, and a street runs through the village. This deserted village is unusual in that its alignment changed. The later settlement, with a street aligned towards the viewer, was superimposed on the earlier one which runs almost horizontally across this photograph. Traces of both villages can be seen in the surviving earthworks.

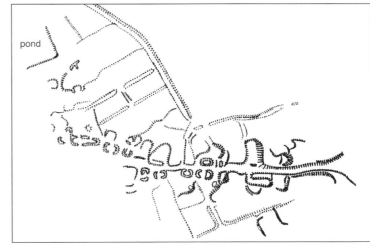

21. Parch-marks, Shapwick. Parch-marks in grass reveal the location of several ring-ditches, which are generally presumed to be the surviving remains of barrows (prehistoric burial mounds). The mounds themselves seem to have been plough-ed away, but a long period of dry weather has caused the grass over the ditches surrounding the mounds to die. The ditches appear here as pale circles in the grass. Paradoxically, in less extreme weather conditions the greater relative moisture content of the soil in the ditches allows lusher crop growth and the ditches appear as dark circles in a paler crop.

*22. Crop-marks, Tarrant Monkton
(SW, 20 July 1994)*

*21. Parch-marks, Shapwick
(SW, 31 August 1995)*

22. Tarrant Monkton. In a field of peas, crop-marks of what seems to be a wide bank with a single entrance enclosing a small, almost circular area. Slightly darker growth around the interior of the bank hints at the presence of a ditch, and suggests that this might be a type of henge monument.

Strictly speaking, this feature is too small to be a henge proper, and should be described as a *hengi-form* monument. These monuments are of late Neolithic date and seem to have been used for ritual or ceremonial purposes.

This provisional interpretation is complicated by the fact that peas are known, in certain conditions, to produce pale-coloured crop-marks over deep features such as ditches. As with all crop-marks, further archaeological work would be needed before the nature and date of this previously unrecorded feature could be understood more clearly.

23. Oakley Down and Wor Barrow
(National Monuments Record, 11 July 1967)

Cranborne Chase

Cranborne Chase takes its name from the medieval use of the area as a royal forest in which settlement and other activities were restricted. For archaeologists, however, the richest and most intriguing periods in the area's development are prehistoric. Neolithic and Bronze Age monuments in particular are abundant, and the area has drawn antiquaries and archaeologists for centuries. For example, the Dorset Cursus, then an earthwork crossing the downs, was first observed and recorded by antiquaries in the eighteenth century. The name cursus comes from their mistaken belief that this long, thin enclosure was a prehistoric race course.

General Pitt-Rivers (1827–1900) of Rushmore, a noted antiquary, pioneer of modern archaeological techniques, and the first Inspector of Ancient Monuments, was particularly active in Cranborne Chase. He recorded and excavated many monuments in the area. More recently, the work of local farmer Martin Green, in association with Richard Bradley (University of Reading) and John Barratt (University of Sheffield) in particular, has given us a greater understanding of the enormous complexity of life on Cranborne Chase in prehistoric times, and demonstrated the importance of the study of this area to our understanding of prehistoric Wessex as a whole.

Circular burial features, often in the form of barrows, are a particular feature of the Bronze Age. There are over 2500 barrows in the Dorset Sites & Monuments Record, surviving predominantly in areas of chalk geology, and in particular concentrations in Cranborne Chase and along the Ridgeway in the southern part of the county.

23. Oakley Down and Wor Barrow. This oblique photograph shows the Oakley Down group of barrows; over thirty barrows (prehistoric burial mounds), most lying in the angle between a Roman road and the modern Salisbury to Blandford Forum road. The group includes a number of disc barrows which have a small central mound surrounded by a large flat area, or berm, and an outer bank and ditch. Note the disc barrows here with more than one central mound. There are also a number of bell barrows, with a larger, supposedly bell-shaped mound, as well as the more common bowl barrows. In the background is Wor Barrow (photograph **24**), a Neolithic long barrow which was excavated by General Pitt-Rivers in 1893–94. The earthwork seen here was created by him as an amphitheatre.

24. Wor Barrow
(SW, 11 July 1967)

29

*25. The Dorset Cursus
(FR, October 1972)*

25. Long, narrow enclosures formed by a low bank and external ditch, cursus were built for ceremonial or ritual purposes in the Neolithic period; the elongated shape suggests some sort of procession. There is some archaeological evidence to suggest that cursus may have been used for excarnation, or the exposure of the dead. The Dorset Cursus is approximately 90m wide and just over 10 kilometres (6 miles) long, the largest known. Only a very small part of the cursus survives as an earthwork; for most of its length it can now only be seen as soil- or crop-marks on aerial photographs.

In this photograph the cursus, appearing as two pale parallel lines, crosses from just below the top right to the bottom left corner. It is crossed by the earthworks of a Roman road, Ackling Dyke, seen here as a straight line in the field boundaries at the bottom and running through woodland towards the top of the photograph. Elsewhere, we can see traces of extensive prehistoric field systems and associated settlements, and mounds or chalky marks and dark ring-ditches which are the remains of barrows (though beware: some of the more shapeless pale smudges in this photograph are quite modern and result from the digging of pits for chalk).

*26. Knowlton, Woodlands
(National Monuments Record,
11 July 1969)*

26. Knowlton, Woodlands. The ruined church at Knowlton stands inside one of a cluster of several Neolithic henge monuments, this one known as *Centre Circle* or *Church Henge*. Henge monuments usually consist of a large bank outside a ditch, so cannot have been built for defensive purposes, and are presumed to have fulfilled some kind of ceremonial role. The surviving walls of the church are mainly of flint with ashlar dressings of greensand and heathstone, and parts of the building appear to date from the twelfth century. It seems to have fallen out of use in the late sixteenth century, though according to Hutchins there was a revival of use around 1730. The rectangular enclosure inside the henge is thought to be the old churchyard bank.

31

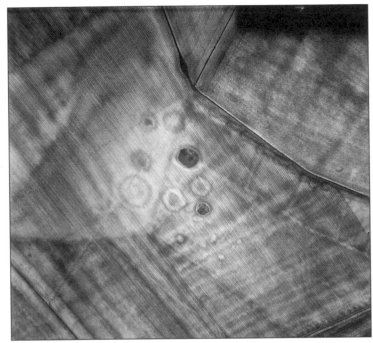

27. Wyke Down, Gussage All Saints
(National Monuments Record, 4 April 1977)

28. Romano-British settlement at Bokerley Junction
(National Monuments Record, 22 April 1976)

27. Wyke Down, Gussage All Saints. Soil-marks and earthworks of a prehistoric field-system and a cluster of barrows. Traces of the mounds of some of the barrows appear as chalky marks, in others dark patches suggest organic deposits and may indicate that the barrow was constructed around a turf core.

28. Part of a Romano-British settlement which lies on both sides of Bokerley Dyke (see below) around Bokerley Junction, the point where the Roman road from Old Sarum to Dorchester crosses the Dyke. The Roman road survives as an earthwork, leaving the top left-hand corner of this photograph. The settlement was partly excavated by General Pitt-Rivers in 1888–90 and by Philip Rahtz in 1958. Excavated features included enclosures, hearths and ovens, numerous pits, and burials; finds suggest that the main period of occupation was AD 275–400.

29. Cranborne (DCC, 21 July 1997)

29. Cranborne Chase takes its name from the small town of Cranborne, on the River Crane. A monastery was founded here around 980, and a settlement gradually developed. The Domesday Book entry shows that Cranborne had become a royal manor by 1086; later it was granted by William Rufus to Robert fitz Hamon, who removed all but a prior and two monks from Cranborne to augment the community at Tewkesbury Abbey, which he refounded in 1102. King John acquired the manor through marriage, and had the manor house rebuilt as a hunting lodge in 1207–8. The house was acquired at the beginning of the seventeenth century by Robert Cecil, first earl of Salisbury, who had it restored and thereby preserved much of the earlier building within the fabric of the present house.

Prominent in this photograph are the present gardens of Cranborne Manor (bottom left quarter), which have their origins in formal gardens planned at this time. The present settlement of Cranborne has much the same layout as it did in the medieval period, with roads converging to cross the stream at a point near the church.

During the twelfth and thirteenth centuries increasing population pressure led to encroachment upon royal forests. Cranborne Chase was no exception. The number of single farmsteads increased, each becoming the focus of a steadily-expanding area of cultivated land.

33

30. Mount Pleasant, West Stafford
(FR, 2 March 1997)

Monuments

There are around ten thousand sites in the Dorset Sites & Monuments Record. Many of them were identified through the examination of aerial photographs.

The Sites & Monuments Record (SMR) was established in 1972 and is located at County Hall in Dorchester. It is a register of all known archaeological sites and historic landscape features in Dorset. Sites in the SMR range from isolated finds or fragments of pottery to massive earthwork features covering many acres; from the earliest prehistoric periods to World War II defences. Wrecks and underwater sites are also recorded.

Information comes from a variety of sources: aerial photographs, books and journals, from landowners and members of the public, as well as reports from local amateur groups and professional archaeologists. The SMR is expanding and being updated constantly.

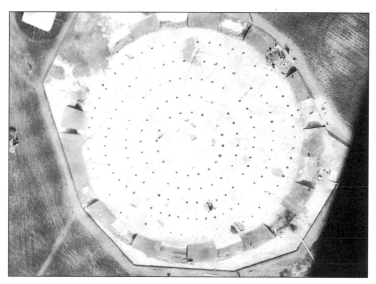

31. Mount Pleasant timber structure during excavation (R.N.R. Peers, August 1970)

30, 31. Mount Pleasant, West Stafford, is one of a number of large monuments which were built in the Neolithic in the area now occupied by Dorchester. These include Maumbury Rings and a curious arc of massive post-holes discovered during excavations in the centre of Dorchester. At Mount Pleasant a bank with an internal ditch encloses the hill top. The clump of woodland on the far edge of the monument is a probable Bronze Age barrow known as Conquer Barrow; we very often see continuity of interest in particular sites for burial or ceremonial purposes from the Neolithic into the Bronze Age. On excavation, the henge monument was found to enclose a structure composed of concentric circles of holes, presumed to be for timber posts, and seen above (**31**) during excavation in August 1970.

33. Cerne Abbas Giant. This chalk figure is widely and popularly associated with Dorset. There are a number of theories about its meaning and origin. Chalk figures from other parts of the country have been shown to be late prehistoric in date. Some authorities feel that a resemblance to Hercules suggests that the figure may be Romano-British, and that a late prehistoric or Romano-British date is likely. Others find it difficult to believe that an overtly pagan image such as this could have survived the medieval period intact, particularly as the earliest known documentary reference to the figure is a note in local parish records of a sum paid for materials in the seventeenth century. A popular explanation of the Giant's origin is that he was constructed in the seventeenth century on the orders of local magnate Denzil Holles as a gesture of defiance to Cromwell.

The Giant has been repaired and recut a number of times. He was not, as many suppose, created by cutting down to the natural chalk, but by cutting a shallow trench which was then packed with imported chalk. Some parts of the figure, for example the nose, are built up into turf-covered mounds.

34. The Giant found a mate briefly in 1997 when, as an experiment in surveying methods, students from the School of Conservation Sciences at Bournemouth University set out a female figure near by.

32. Maumbury Rings, Dorchester
(National Monuments Record, 2 February 1971)

32. Maumbury Rings. This Neolithic henge monument lies preserved between the Weymouth to Bristol and the Weymouth to London railway lines. Public alarm caused the line, which would have damaged the monument severely, to be moved. This monument was modified to serve as an amphitheatre for Roman Dorchester, *Durnovaria*, and during the civil war in the seventeenth century to form a strong point in the town's defences.

33. Cerne Abbas Giant
(SW, 21 August 1995)

34. Cerne Giant and Giantess
(FR, 1997)

35. The Kingston Russell stone circle
(FR, 3 March 1990)

35. Fallen stones of the Kingston Russell stone circle, an irregular oval approximately 22 metres by 30 metres. The largest
stone is over 2 metres high. Small stone circles such as this one
were generally built in the early Bronze Age. Note the storm
damage in the plantation towards the back of this photograph.

38

36. Lulworth Cove and Bindon Hill (FR, 17 August 1994)

36. Lulworth Cove and Bindon Hill. Aerial photographs help us to see just how much work must have gone in to constructing the earthworks on Bindon Hill. A small amount of excavation work has been carried out here, enough to show that these earthworks were built in the Iron Age; first a bank and ditch enclosing a large area which included Lulworth Cove, then another bank and ditch around to top of Bindon Hill itself, and a later cross-ridge dyke across the hill. The overall impression given by the earthworks is that they face inland, perhaps to protect the cove.

37. Barrows, Sixpenny Handley
(FR, 24 April 1990)

Boundaries

Many Dorset parishes coincide with Saxon estates. The estates were often referred to in Anglo-Saxon charters which contain boundary clauses in Old English, giving the extent of estates. There are frequent references to prehistoric monuments which were adopted as boundary markers since they were then, as now, prominent landscape features.

37. Barrows, Sixpenny Handley. Part of the parish boundary between Sixpenny Handley and Gussage All Saints. The large barrow in the angle of the boundary is thought to be the *Berendes beorh*, or Berend's Barrow, referred to in a charter of 956 which sets out the Handley estate boundaries.

*38. Bokerley Dyke
(National Monuments Record, 16 February 1989)*

38. Bokerley Dyke. A massive ditch which, for much of its length, corresponds to the modern county boundary. The name *Bokerley* is relatively modern, and comes from the use of part of the dyke as a deer-park boundary in the medieval period. It was once thought that the dyke was built at a time of unrest at the end of the Roman period, but excavation and study of the relationships between this and other boundaries in the area suggest that the first dyke was constructed in the Bronze Age. The northern end of The Dorset Cursus can be seen as a soil-mark in the foreground. In the foreground are two long barrows.

*39. Hambledon Hill
(DCC, August 1997)*

*40. (inset) Neolithic causewayed
enclosure, Hambledon Hill
(DCC, August 1997)*

Hill-forts

Hill-forts were built in the Iron Age and, as their name suggests, were invariably constructed in positions which had a certain natural prominence. Nevertheless, even the simplest of them represents an enormous investment of time and effort by the local population and considerable organisation to co-ordinate the work. Most began as a simple enclosure with a single bank and ditch. Some never developed beyond this, but others were elaborated with additional banks and ditches, and complex entrance arrangements.

39, 40. Hambledon Hill. The most prominent features here is the Iron Age hill-fort, the ramparts of which enclose the three spurs of Hambledon Hill. This complex hill-fort certainly seems to represent the most intense period of the hill's occupation; the interior was densely crowded and the results of recent survey work hint at an element of planning in the layout of settlement inside the fort. The hill-fort partly conceals traces of earlier activity. There are two Neolithic causewayed enclosures on Hambledon Hill, one on the central part and a smaller one on the south-eastern spur of the hill. The central causewayed enclosure (**41**) survives in places as a slight earthwork, but much of it has been ploughed and its full extent is best appreciated from aerial photographs. The hill-fort itself had several stages of development, and later activity is represented by cross-ridge dykes, traces of medieval cultivation and post-medieval quarries around the edges of the hill which in places cut into the ramparts of the fort.

41. Abbotsbury Castle
(FR, 10 January 1992)

41. Abbotsbury Castle hill-fort on Wears Hill encloses an area of just under 2 hectares. There are double ramparts on the north, south and east sides, but the south-eastern end (back right in this photograph) has four ramparts, formed by later additions. In this shot the low winter sun has thrown up some of the internal features of the hill-fort. A mound, thought to be a Bronze Age barrow, can be seen within the hill-fort, as can a number of circular banks about 6 metres in diameter which have been interpreted as hut circles.

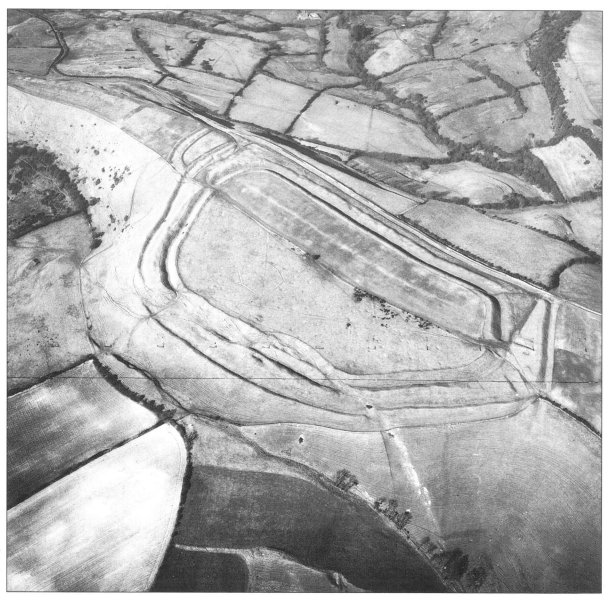

42. Eggardon Hill (National Monuments Record, 16 March 1972)

42. Eggardon hill-fort lies partly in Powerstock and partly in Askerswell parish. This photograph shows how different farming regimes have affected the monument. The parish boundary runs across the monument. On the northern side of the parish boundary (at the top here), where ploughing has been more frequent, the internal features of the fort are blurred. The small octagonal enclosure is relatively modern, the site of a coppice which may have been planted to serve as a sea-mark.

43. Spetisbury Rings
(SW, 20 July 1994)

44. Chalbury, Bincombe
(SW, 21 August 1995)

43. Spetisbury Rings is also known as Crawford Castle. It is an univallate hill-fort with a single entrance to the north-west. The eastern edge of the hill-fort (on the right in this photograph) was partly destroyed in 1857 when the railway was built. The navvies found many skeletons (some accounts say over eighty one year, and forty the next) in a mass grave. The objects found with them included spear heads, swords, torcs, currency bars and brooches, all thought by the finders to be of late Iron Age date (though some of these objects are now thought to be Saxon), and led to speculation that these might have been casualties of an encounter with the advancing Roman army.

44. Chalbury hill-fort, Bincombe, encloses a prominent knoll at the northern end of a ridge overlooking Weymouth, a naturally strong position. The defences of the fort consist of a single rampart and outer ditch, with a single rampart at the south-east end (right foreground). A line of quarry pits runs along the inside of the rampart, and there are circular features, probably hut circles, in the parched interior of the fort.

*45. Rawlesbury Camp
(FR, 7 September 1991)*

45. Rawlesbury Camp, Stoke Wake. A small hill-fort which is situated on a prominent spur jutting out from the chalk escarpment. This photograph shows how steeply the ground falls away; full advantage was taken of this natural slope in building the hill-fort. The ramparts consist of two banks with outer ditches. On the northern site (foreground) there is a flat area, or berm, between the two ramparts. It is thought that the fort was built in two stages, with the inner rampart a later addition. The single entrance is on the left-hand side of this photograph.

*46. Maiden Castle
(DCC, July 1997)*

46. Maiden Castle occupies a chalk hill-top overlooking the rivers Frome and South Winterborne. The hill-top was first cleared of woodland in the Neolithic period around 4000 BC and soon after a causewayed enclosure, two concentric ditches constructed in a series of irregular segments, was built on the eastern part of the hill. After the causewayed enclosure fell out of use, a bank barrow was built across the hill top, a mound 546 metres long, which may have developed from an earlier long barrow. Bowl barrows and a small enclosure suggest that occupation continued into the Bronze Age.

47. The Iron Age hill-fort which overlies the Neolithic and Bronze Age features began as a single rampart with an outer ditch and timber gates. It was extended and remodelled several times, and in its final form had three banks and two ditches around the perimeter of the hill, and an extra bank and ditch along the southern edge. The entrances are particularly complex; here we see the western entrance. Excavation revealed evidence of intensive occupation – traces of circular and rectangular huts, roads, storage pits and ovens – and Maiden Castle was clearly one of the major centres of the local tribe, the *Durotriges.*

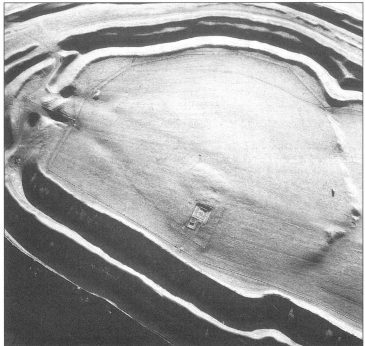

48. Use of Maiden Castle continued in the Roman period, in the form of a Romano-Celtic temple built during the fourth century. The outlines of the temple – a central block surrounded by a corridor or verandah inside a walled precinct – can be seen in this photograph.

*48. The eastern end of Maiden Castle with Roman temple
(National Monuments Record, 6 December 1984)*

49. Dorchester (DCC)

Towns and Villages

Aerial photographs make it particularly easy to appreciate the elements of a settlement's modern form which are pointers to its history and development. Many towns were established in the Roman period, but as yet no evidence has been found to demonstrate any continuity of settlement into later periods. However, the Romans chose good sites for their towns and many were reused. Nearly every town and village in Dorset had its origins in the medieval period, if not earlier. Sometimes there is documentary or cartographic evidence to fill out the picture of the development of a settlement.

49. The county town is something of an exception, in that the origins of Dorchester as a town lie in the Roman period, though there seem to have been prehistoric settlements in the area, in particular at Fordington (in the bottom left of this photograph) and an area to the south-west near Maiden Castle (**50**). The Roman name of Dorchester is generally thought to have been *Durnovaria*. The first construction here after the conquest in AD 43 was almost certainly military: a fort to control the crossing over the River Frome, and probably on a site later occupied by the town's medieval castle and now by the prison. The line of the Roman defences is revealed by the tree-lined walks which enclose the town centre. The first defences were built in the second century and consisted of an earth bank and ditch. Later elaborations included the fourth-century addition of a stone wall, part of which survives near the Top O'Town roundabout.

Several stone building complexes have been excavated in Colliton Park, in the north-western corner of the Roman town, now occupied by County Hall. One of these buildings, the Roman town-house, is preserved in the grounds of County Hall. As Roman administration disintegrated, the town fell into disuse and decay. Though there was sporadic occupation and use of the area, Dorchester did not flourish again as a town until the Saxon and medieval periods, and even then much of the area inside the Roman walls was not built up.

50. The Romano-British settlement between Dorchester and Maiden Castle (FR, 22 September 1991)

51. Bridport
(National
Monuments Record,
8 May 1989)

51. Bridport stands on a low promontory at the confluence of the rivers Brit, Simene and Asker. The town does not take its name from the river, but from the Old English for 'harbour or market town belonging to Bredy'. The oldest part of the town is the area of South Street (running down the centre of the photograph) around St Mary's church. The street plan suggests that later a suburb was laid out with West Street/East Street (running horizontally across the top of the photograph) as a wide market street with regular burgage plots. The suburban extension is thought to have taken place in the thirteenth century.

The town's prosperity came from the rope industry, which was well established by the early thirteenth century. Hemp and flax came from all over West Dorset for manufacture in Bridport. In 1213 the town was threatened by King John because production was too low. In places the long, narrow plots of ropewalks, in which lengths of rope were twisted, can be seen.

52. West Bay now serves as a harbour for Bridport. Early maps and documents suggest that the harbour was situated on the river and closer to the town in the medieval period.

53. Whitcombe. A shrunken medieval village, which now consists only of the church, a farm, and a few cottages surrounded by the earthworks of former dwellings and their adjoining plots of land. The dedication of the parish church is not known. Tenth-century carved stones inside the building hint at an early origin for the church and settlement. Traces of thirteenth-century wall paintings survive inside the church. A prominent feature of the farmyard is a large seventeenth-century barn.

52. West Bay, Bridport (SW, 15 September 1997)

53. Whitcombe (FR, 30 July 1992)

54. Cerne Abbas. This small town in West Dorset grew up around the abbey after which it is named, and upon which its economy largely depended. Names such as *Webbe, Touker* (a version of *Fuller*, commonly used in the South West) and *Deyher* recorded in the Lay Subsidy Roll of 1332 suggest the existence of a small cloth industry. Earthworks in the background of this photograph are part of the abbey. In the left foreground is a tithe barn which was built in the mid-fourteenth century.

55. Ashmore. The village is centred upon a large round pond from which it takes its name, since Ashmore is thought to come from the Old English for 'pool where ash trees grow'. Ashmore is situated rather untypically for a Dorset village on a spur over-looking two valleys and at a height of over 200 metres above sea-level. Some authorities have felt that this location, similar to that of a number of Romano-British settlements in the vicinity, hints at an early origin for the village.

54. Cerne Abbas
(SW, 21 August 1995)

55. Ashmore
(National Monuments Record, March 1968)

56. Hinton St Mary, house and church
(SW, 13 July 1994)

57. Shapwick
(SW, 28 July 1994)

56. Hinton St Mary. The village has grown up around the parish church and the manor house and its gardens. The west tower of St Peter's church is fifteenth century, but most of the rest of the building was rebuilt in 1846. A medieval barn survives and the manor house incorporates a number of medieval elements, including a thirteenth-century hall, but is largely seventeenth century with later enlargements and alterations.

57. Shapwick. The name of this village on the banks of the river Stour comes from the Old English for 'sheep farm'. Expansion of the settlement was inhibited by the open field system around the village, which remained unenclosed until 1813, and this photograph shows how the village has retained the compact form which it had in the medieval period. Some parts of the parish church of St Bartholomew (in the centre of the photograph) are twelfth century, though it is mostly fourteenth century, and was restored in 1878.

58. St Catherine's Chapel, Abbotsbury
(National Monuments Record, 28 August 1987)

Churches

In general parish churches were established close to a castle or manor house by local lords. The earliest churches tended to be wooden, and to be replaced by buildings in local materials. Many were built or rebuilt by the Normans. In the later Middle Ages wealthy parishes or individual parishioners might import stone for additions and alterations to the parish church. Complete rebuilding in any one period was rare; sporadic additions and reconstructions mean that today's parish churches are usually a mixture of styles. Many were subject to at least partial (sometimes rather heavy-handed) restoration in the Victorian period.

58. St Catherine's Chapel stands on a hill just to the south-west of Abbotsbury village. The chapel was built of local rubble and ashlar by the abbey of Abbotsbury in the late fourteenth century. In this photograph medieval cultivation terraces or strip lynchets are emphasised by slight shadows.

59. Bere Regis was an important market town with strong royal connections in the medieval period. King John had a house built here, and the town was made into a free borough by Edward I. The medieval centre was destroyed by a succession of fires in the post-medieval period and the oldest surviving domestic buildings now date from around 1600. The open fields around the village were not enclosed until 1846, and many of the houses here were originally built as small farmhouses.

This photograph shows the parish church in the heart of the village. The present parish church of St John the Baptist incorporates the remains of a church of around 1050. The development of the building since that time has been complex. Prominent elements of the present building are the imposing tower and the roof of the nave, built around 1500.

59. Bere Regis (FR, 30 May 1992)

60. Stourpaine. The Domesday Book entry suggests that there were a number of settlements in Stourpaine parish in the early medieval period. These settlements along the River Iwerne included Lazerton and Ash, as well as Stourpaine itself. Now all but Stourpaine are much reduced. The parish church of the Holy Trinity was rebuilt in 1858, with only the fifteenth-century west tower surviving from earlier periods. In the foreground of this photograph are the earthworks of one of Dorset's few medieval moated sites.

60. Stourpaine (SW, 1994)

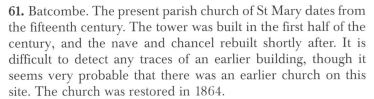

62. Iwerne Minster
(SW, 13 July 1994)

61. Batcombe
(FR, 21 February 1992)

61. Batcombe. The present parish church of St Mary dates from the fifteenth century. The tower was built in the first half of the century, and the nave and chancel rebuilt shortly after. It is difficult to detect any traces of an earlier building, though it seems very probable that there was an earlier church on this site. The church was restored in 1864.

62. Iwerne Minster is situated on the River Iwerne. This is a Celtic river name, perhaps the name of a goddess, or referring to yew trees. There was a minster here and Iwerne Minster was already a large settlement by the time of the Domesday Survey. The parish church of St Mary incorporates the remains of a twelfth-century building, and was subject to a number of alterations and additions. The present tower was built in the fourteenth century, but its appearance changed considerably in the nineteenth century, when the octagonal spire was altered and reduced in height. The church was restored by T.H. Wyatt in 1871.

63. Winterborne Farringdon is one of several deserted or shrunken medieval villages which lie along the River Winterborne south of Dorchester. Here the sole upstanding building is the gable end of St German's church in a small churchyard enclosure. In this photograph earthworks of house platforms and boundaries throw long shadows in a low winter light, and in places there are signs of small-scale quarrying. Gradual depopulation of the village seems to have begun as early as the thirteenth century. The village was not taxed in 1428 because there were less than ten inhabitants, and from 1580 the same incumbent served St German's and the neighbouring church of Winterborne Came. In 1773 Hutchins wrote that Farringdon 'is entirely depopulated and has been so beyond the memory of man'.

63. Winterborne Farringdon
(FR, 8 November 1991)

64. Bradford Peverell. The parish church of St Mary was rebuilt in 1850 to the designs of Decimus Burton, but retains some fittings from the older church.

*64. Bradford Peverell
(FR, 18 July 1996)*

65. The parish church of St Mary seems to have been rebuilt in the late fifteenth century, and again in the 1850s, though the fifteenth-century tower survives and medieval windows were retained. Some evidence of a pre-Conquest church is to be found inside the present church: part of a tenth- or eleventh-century pillar carved with a continuous design of beasts and interlace decoration, adapted for use as a font.

*65. Melbury Bubb
(FR, 6 April 1997)*

66. Witchampton. At the time of the Domesday Survey Witchampton and East and West Hemsworth were substantial settlements. Now only Witchampton remains as a settlement; East and West Hemsworth are simple farms. The area known as 'New Town', about 800 metres north-east of the village, was established in the eighteenth century. The parish church is dedicated to St Mary, St Cuthberga and All Saints.

66. Witchampton village and church
(SW, 8 September 1994)

67. The large parish of Charminster once contained several small hamlets or farmsteads, as well as the main settlement of Charminster itself, strung along the River Cerne. The parish church of St Mary the Virgin has a magnificent sixteenth-century tower.

67. Charminster village centre and church
(SW, 21 August 1995)

68. Smacam Down
(FR, 15 July 1991)

Fields and Farms

There is a growing recognition of the continuity of land use and the gradual evolution of field systems. For example, the large organised field systems which covered much of the later prehistoric landscape seem to have continued in use and suffered little disruption following the Roman invasion. Some elements of these early systems were incorporated into later systems and in some cases survive as part of modern field boundaries. The origin of common or open field systems is not clear, but they seem to have developed in some places at the same time as the first nucleated villages. A feature of open field systems is their division into long, narrow 'strips'. The land was cultivated jointly, to make the best use of scarce resources. One manifestation of this system is the slightly-curving S-shaped earthworks of 'ridge and furrow', now much depleted in Dorset by later farming activities. Towards the end of the Middle Ages and in post-medieval periods communal systems gradually disintegrated and land was enclosed. In some places, enclosure took place by agreement, in others, by Act of Parliament. The first Parliamentary Enclosure Act was in 1605 for the enclosure of land at Radipole near Weymouth.

68. Smacam Down, Cerne Abbas. Earthworks of a prehistoric farmstead surrounded by an extensive field system which has barrows incorporated into the boundaries. These systems of regular fields are often called 'Celtic' field systems, which can be confusing. They are certainly prehistoric in origin. Evidence from excavations suggests that field systems like these on Smacam Down were first constructed in the later Bronze Age, and may have continued in use right through the Iron Age and into the Roman period. The very regular appearance of the field boundaries in some areas suggests that they may have been laid out in one go, in a planned effort, while other areas are less coherent.

69. Grimston Down, Stratton. Earthworks of a once-extensive prehistoric field system which still covers over 30 hectares. Several trackways, one particularly prominent in the centre of this photograph, converge on a cluster of smaller enclosures which is probably a settlement.

69. Grimston Down
(FR, 14 January 1990)

70. Ringmoor, Turnworth
(FR, 19 March 1995)

Ringmoor, Turnworth. The layout of the prehistoric settlement and field systems on Ringmoor is particularly easy to see in this oblique photograph (**70**), as earthworks are thrown into relief by a low sun. A prominent feature in this shot is a trackway which runs diagonally across the spur. In the centre of these fields and trackways is a small enclosure, seen in close-up in the next photograph (**71**).

Small, irregular fields with thick hedgerows like those in photograph **72**, known as assarts, are thought to be the result of the gradual clearance of woodland around newly-established farmsteads in the medieval period.

71. Ringmoor enclosure
(National Monuments Record, 9 May 1994)

72. Assarts
(DCC)

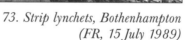

*73. Strip lynchets, Bothenhampton
(FR, 15 July 1989)*

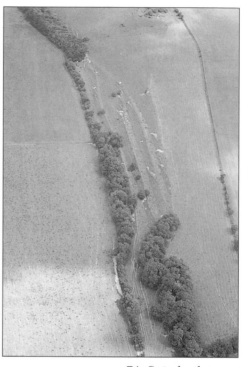

*74. Strip lynchets east
of Fontmell Magna
(SW, 13 July 1994)*

Strip lynchets (medieval cultivation terraces) are a familiar feature of the hilly countryside in the western part of Dorset. They were constructed to facilitate ploughing on difficult sloping ground. In photograph **73**, lynchets curve around a hillside at Bonscombe, Bothenhampton, and **74** shows others near Fontmell Magna.

Water-meadows comprise a system of ridges and channels constructed to allow grassland to be artificially flooded at certain times of year in order to produce early, good quality pasture. In photograph **75** unusually heavy rain has filled the channels at Throop with water, which enables us to see the structure of the system more clearly. This system, on the River Frome, could be of seventeenth- or eighteenth-century date.

Photograph **77** shows a farmer meeting the harvest-time challenge presented by a curiously shaped field at Lake, near Wimborne. The slight linear earthwork in the field to the right of the star-shaped field is a Roman road, the road from Badbury Rings to the Roman fort and settlement (in the area at the top left of this photograph) at Lake and on to Hamworthy.

75. Water-meadows, Throop (SW, 15 February 1995)

76. Large fields and cylindrical
bales: a common feature
of the modern Dorset landscape
(FR, July 1995)

77. Star-shaped field
(National Monuments Record, 11 July 1969)

78. Wimborne Minster
(National Monuments Record, 21 June 1993)

Monasteries

Early monasteries in Britain were destroyed by Viking invaders in the eighth and ninth centuries. Wessex was the scene of a revival of British monasticism in the tenth and eleventh centuries. By AD 1000 Benedictine houses had been founded or refounded at places such as Glastonbury, Shaftesbury, and Winchester. The Rule of St Benedict, the cardinal principle of which was obedience, established the pattern of monastic life. Monasteries were generally large establishments, and had a profound effect on local economies and settlement patterns. The explosion in monastic growth had come to an end by the mid-thirteenth century, and by the fourteenth century monasteries were in decline. The Black Death depleted monastic communities, and the population in general, leading to a drop in endowments. At the same time, there was an increasing tendency for people to favour their parish churches, for example by endowing a chantry chapel, rather than the monasteries. Decline continued and Henry VIII met little resistance when he closed all 650 monasteries in England and Wales in the period between 1536 and 1540, and confiscated their property.

78. Wimborne Minster. The name Wimborne comes from the Old English *Winn* plus *burna*, meaning 'at the bright stream' or 'meadow stream'. King Ine founded a double monastery here around 705, an establishment for monks and nuns, governed by an abbess. Wimborne was also a royal residence and, according to the Anglo-Saxon Chronicle, the scene of a rising by the atheling Ethelwold in AD 900. The present Minster is the successor to the monastery. Traces of Saxon stonework can be seen in the present building, which has twelfth-, thirteenth-, and fifteenth-century additions, and was considerably restored in the 1840s. The early town was confined to a small area in the vicinity of the Minster, but later expanded northwards along

East and West Borough (foreground). The earthworks of a planned suburb of around 1200 can be seen on The Leaze (back right).

79, 80. Abbotsbury Abbey. The date of foundation of the Benedictine abbey is uncertain, but it may have been refounded by Orc in the early eleventh century, since the first documentary reference to an abbey here seems to be a grant to St Peter's Abbotsbury by Orc's widow between 1058 and 1066. Little survives of the abbey, though the outline of part of the abbey church can be seen in the churchyard south of the parish church, also St Peter's. Part of the tithe barn and one gatehouse remain in use.

An eleventh-century document refers to the establishment of a guild in Abbotsbury. The Abbotsbury guild is an interesting example of a corporate organisation of a religious nature, founded to commemorate Orc and his wife Tola. Pre-Conquest guilds are known only from a handful of towns. In the later medieval period a guild was a religious organisation composed of men and women working at a single craft and living and working in the same parish.

The later development of Abbotsbury depended heavily upon the abbey. The town was never a borough, and declined somewhat following the Dissolution of the Monasteries. The abbey passed to Giles Strangways, who built a house of stone from the abbey ruins. During the Civil War Sir John Strangways raised two companies of townsmen to support the Royalist cause. His house, next to the church, was attacked and blown up in 1644. Most of the buildings in the centre are seventeenth century.

81. (above) Shaftesbury
(National Monuments Record, 3 March 1970)

79. (top left) Abbotsbury (FR, 14 October 1996)
80. (left) Abbotsbury (FR, 14 October 1996)

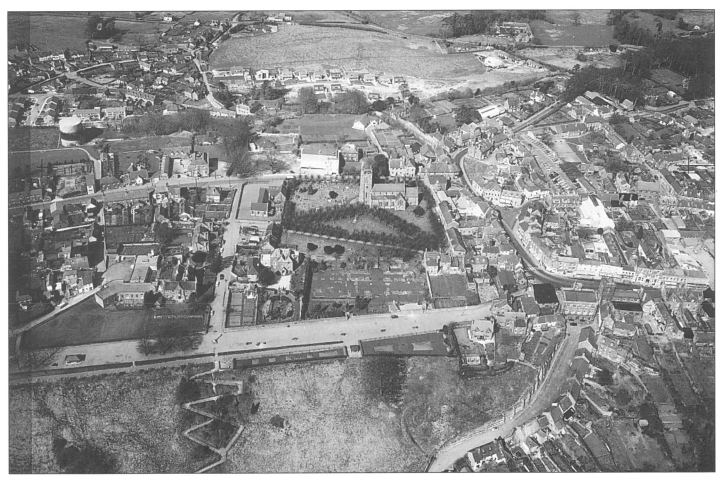

*82. Close-up of Shaftesbury Abbey
(National Monuments Record, 3 March 1970)*

81, 82. Shaftesbury. The town occupies a dramatic exposed site on a steep-sided Greensand promontory overlooking the Blackmore Vale. In the left foreground (**81**) are the earthworks of Castle Hill, thought to be a temporary fortification thrown up during the civil war of the twelfth century. Shaftesbury Abbey was founded by King Alfred for his daughter Æthelgeofu, the first abbess, and the abbey dominated the town and its economy for centuries. Though the abbey declined in the later medieval period, it nevertheless had fifty-five nuns when it was dissoved in 1539. After the Dissolution the abbey buildings were quarried for building stone and quickly ruined.

83. Sherborne Abbey (National Monuments Record, 21 June 1993)

83. Sherborne Abbey. Sherborne sits on the north bank of the river Yeo, and its name comes from the Old English *scir* plus *burna*, meaning 'meadow stream' or 'at the bright stream'. There is much evidence of Iron Age and Romano-British occupation here, but the present layout of the town is largely the result of the powerful influence of Sherborne Abbey. The abbey, seen here from the south, stands in the middle of the town. A cathedral was first built at Sherborne in the early 700s, and the Saxon kings Ethelbald and Ethelbert are buried here. There are a few traces of the pre-Conquest church in the present building. Considerable rebuilding was undertaken in the twelfth century, with many later additions and alterations. Parts of the church were burnt following a riot in 1437, stimulating further major reconstruction. Following the Dissolution the buildings were sold, partly dismantled, and the church fell into disrepair. Many of the abbey buildings are now used by Sherborne School. A general restoration of the church was begun in 1849.

84. Milton Abbey (DCC, 19 October 1972)

84. Milton Abbey. The Benedictine Abbey of St Samson, St Branwallader and the Blessed Virgin Mary was founded by King Athelstan (925–39) who, according to a dubious later charter, gave the abbey relics of the two saints. King Edgar reformed the house in 964. A settlement quickly grew up at the abbey gate. Entries in the Lay Subsidy Roll of 1332 indicate a populous but modest agricultural settlement. The abbey was rebuilt in the fourteenth century, having been destroyed by fire in 1309. The abbot's great hall was finished in 1498. On dissolution the abbey was passed to John Tregonwell and the abbey church became the parish church.

Milton Abbey House (top left quarter of the photograph), incorporating the abbey buildings, was created around 1771 by Sir William Chambers for Joseph Damer, first Baron Milton, later earl of Dorchester. Between 1771 and 1790 Baron Milton removed the town to create a landscape park. A new model village was created to the east of the original town to house the population, a single street of houses running from the centre to the right of this photograph. Capability Brown was employed to plan the landscaping of the park, which at its largest covered 3000 acres. A prominent feature of the scheme is a grassy stairway which rises through woodland east of the abbey to St Catherine's Chapel.

85. Portland
(DCC, July 1997)

Portland and the Fleet

85. For most of its history, Portland has been joined to the mainland only by the massive shingle bank known as Chesil Beach. A bridge over the Fleet was built in 1839 and a railway in 1865.

Little is known about the early history of settlement on Portland. There is much evidence of intense activity from the Mesolithic to the Roman period. On the southern part of the island in particular, extensive Mesolithic occupation remains survive. A peculiar feature of the Iron Age/Romano-British period on Portland are 'beehive' chambers which were excavated in some numbers in advance of quarrying in the late nineteenth and early twentieth centuries.

Portland was a royal manor in Saxon times. It was granted to Winchester Abbey by Henry I and returned to the Crown in the fifteenth century. The open strip fields, known locally as *lawnsheds*, have survived in some areas in almost continuous use to the present day and are particularly well preserved on the southern part of the island around Portland Bill.

The Jurassic rocks of which Portland is made produce fine building stone, but this was not widely exploited until relatively recently because the finer stones lay under a great depth of overburden. An export trade developed in the seventeenth century, and the shores of the island bristle with quays and jetties from which the stone was removed.

Rufus Castle and St Andrew's church, situated together on the east cliffs, are the only surviving medieval buildings on Portland. Rufus Castle was built in the fifteenth century. Though it has all the appearance of a medieval castle, and despite its other name of 'Bow and Arrow Castle', Rufus Castle was designed as an early artillery fort.

86. By contrast, Portland Castle (built 1539–40) is very unlike a medieval castle. In a short period from 1539 Henry VIII

86. Portland Castle
(National Monuments Record, 25 July 1996)

built a series of artillery forts along the south coast to guard against the threat of invasion from the continent. Portland Castle is on the east coast at the point where Chesil Beach joins Portland, and was situated to command the deep water anchorage between Weymouth and Portland. It was built for £4964.19s. 10¹⁄₄d. The main part of the building is a two-storey keep housing the garrison and stores, with guns behind a parapet on the roof. On the seaward side was a single-storey gun room with guns on the roof and slits for more guns on the floor below. Portland Castle and Sandsfoot Castle between them commanded the approaches to the harbour.

87. The Verne
(National Monuments Record,
7 August 1923)

87. The Verne was built between 1852 and 1867, one of a number of forts built to combat the threat of invasion by the French. The massive ramparts and deep ditches are a reflection of the need to minimise damage caused by the increasingly heavy shells carried by the new iron-clad warships. Such forts had a low-profile, thick earthen ramparts and below-ground storage and accommodation. The fort's own defences were by no means modest: its 38-ton guns had a field of fire in all directions and a 10-mile range.

Stone excavated during the construction of the Verne was used to complete the massive breakwaters which turned Portland Harbour into a huge deep-water anchorage. Convict labour from the newly established prison was used for this work.

The breakwater defences were extended in 1902 and 1904, to enclose the whole harbour. Further security was added by the construction of the Breakwater Fort and the sinking of HMS *Hood* in the approaches to the southern harbour in 1914. The fortifications of the Verne played an important part in the World War II defences of southern Dorset. .

The Coast

88. Lyme Regis (DCC, 21 September 1997)

89. Charmouth (DCC)

88. Lyme Regis. The early history of Lyme is not clear. The Domesday Book entry shows that saltworking was important, and there may have been a small fishing and saltworking settlement here, now destroyed by coastal erosion. The church has some twelfth-century features, and might perhaps have been the focus for early settlement. Lyme was well established by 1284, when a charter of Edward I made it a free borough and created a merchant guild. A decline began in the fourteenth century when the town suffered much from landslips and storms. The sixteenth century saw a gradual revival as the port developed extensive trading connections, but the town was again in decline by the mid-eighteenth century. Lyme's fortunes rose from around 1760 as a vogue for sea bathing took hold and it became a resort. This vertical photograph shows how the development of the town has been constrained by topography. A particularly prominent feature of the the coastline at Lyme is The Cobb, a stone pier forming a harbour. The first Cobb was probably built in the later thirteenth century. In its present form, it is much repaired and extended, but almost certainly follows the line of the original structure.

89. Charmouth. In the early medieval period the prosperity of Charmouth seems to have depended upon salt production. In 1086 the Domesday Survey recorded sixteen saltworkers at Charmouth. Any settlement then was almost certainly situated on the coast, now eroded, rather than nearthe present town. Charmouth is known to have been among the possessions of Forde Abbey by 1189. In 1320 the abbot set about improving Charmouth: a free borough was created and a new town set out along a single main street. The burgage plots were to be 66 feet by 330 feet, and survive in many places as the modern property boundaries seen in this photograph. Since space on the street frontage was at a premium, a characteristic of burgage plots is their long, thin shape. To make the most of this awkward shape, there would generally be a row of outbuildings stretching back from the main building at the front of the plot. Lesser roads run down from the main street to the sea, the source of the town's livelihood.

90. Osmington White Horse
(FR, 22 September 1991)

90. Osmington White Horse. A chalk-cut figure on White Horse Hill was cut in the early 1800s, and represents George III on his charger. The figure was no doubt intended to be viewed from the flourishing resort of Weymouth.

91. Weymouth. The present town encompasses the two towns of Weymouth, to the south of the estuary of the River Wey, and Melcombe Regis to the north. Neither is identified in the Domesday Book, perhaps because they formed part of larger manors at that time. Both seem to have been small ports by the early twelfth century. A planned town was set out at Melcombe Regis around 1280, and traces of the grid layout survive in the present street pattern. In 1348 Melcombe was the point of entry of the Black Death, the effects of which probably contributed greatly to the port's decline. Until around 1600 the northern limit of the town was Conygar ditch, which ran across the promontory at the point where George III's statue now stands. In 1571 an Act of Parliament joined Weymouth and Melcome Regis, and the first bridge across the harbour was built in 1597.

After 1600 the town gradually expanded northwards. Weymouth suffered greatly in the Civil War and was besieged 1644–5. Nevertheless, Weymouth was the largest urban centre in Dorset in the seventeenth century, trading cloth widely on the continent and establishing links with Newfoundland. Fires destroyed much of Melcombe Regis in 1665 and Weymouth in 1673. Poole prospered at the expense of Weymouth, drawing away much of the port's Newfoundland trade.

Like Lyme Regis, Weymouth's fortunes rose with the growth of a fashion for sea bathing. It developed as a resort in the late eighteenth century and continued to prosper through royal and aristocratic patronage. As the new resort expanded along the bay, the old commercial town decayed. Further residential expansion was stimulated by the establishment of a naval base at Portland in 1845 and the coming of the railway in 1857.

91. Weymouth (DCC)

92. The Fleet
(FR, 7 March 1991)

92. The Fleet. A long shot of Chesil Beach with Portland in the distance. In the foreground is Abbotsbury Swannery and a small diamond-shaped piece of water which is a duck decoy. Duck decoys originated in Holland and were introduced into Britain in the seventeenth century. The Abbotsbury decoy was constructed in 1655, and was one of the first established in the country. The parallel banks immediately north of the swannery are probably late eighteenth-century irrigation works.

*93. Jordan Hill Roman Temple
(FR, 17 August 1994)*

*94. Prehistoric field systems at Durdle Door thrown
into relief by low light (FR, 17 August 1994)*

*95. St Aldhelm's Chapel, Worth Matravers
(FR, 4 June 1998)*

95. St Aldhelm's Chapel was built in the late twelfth century. It occupies a very prominent position on the coast and, despite its rather squat appearance, is visible over long distances from the seaward side. It may therefore have served as a sea mark as well as a chapel or, when first built, have incorporated a feature which acted as a sea mark. The building owes its present appearance to two episodes of restoration in the nineteenth century, the last carried out in 1873 at the behest of Lord Eldon.

96. A long shot of Poole Harbour
(SW, 21 July 1995)

97. Bournemouth town centre
(National Monuments Record, 20 May 1992)

98. Hengistbury Head (DCC)

97. Bournemouth town centre. The town of Bournemouth developed as a resort in the early nineteenth century. In the foreground crowds of bathers cluster around the pier, and a more modern attraction, the Bournemouth International Centre, is at the left-hand edge of this photograph. The nineteenth- and twentieth-century Pleasure Gardens run inland along the Bourne Stream for about 3 km from the front. The Lower Gardens, seen here, were laid out in the 1840s for the Meyrick family under the influence of Decimus Burton, and became town property in 1873. Some of the older trees, mostly conifers, in these Lower Gardens have survived from the original planting scheme.

98. Hengistbury Head. At the beginning of the Mesolithic period, before the sea rose to fill Christchurch Harbour, the ridge now known as Hengistbury Head overlooked a wide, wooded valley and the point where the rivers Stour and Avon joined to flow to a sea which was then some distance away. Rare evidence of Palaeolithic activity has been found here. There seems also to have been considerable activity around Hengistbury Head in the Mesolithic period, with evidence of flint working and meat-processing having been recovered from this and other sites such as those in Mother Siller's Channel.

The safe natural anchorage created as sea levels rose attracted traders from the continent, and in the later prehistoric period a large international port developed on Hengistbury Head. Particularly prominent in this photograph are the two large ramparts which isolated and presumably defended the headland. A series of excavations by Barry Cunliffe of the Oxford University Institute of Archaeology has shown that goods such as amphorae of wine, pottery, and glass were imported through Hengistbury in exchange for metals such as tin and lead from the South West, and probably also local shale and salt. There is also some evidence of metalworking at Hengistbury Head itself. At much the same time another port flourished only a short distance away in Poole Harbour. The port declined after the Roman invasion, as trading links slowly gravitated towards the south east.

99. Christchurch (DCC)

99, 100. Known in Saxon times as *Twinham* or 'the place between the waters', Christchurch lies on a promontory between the rivers Stour and Avon. The modern name was adopted in the medieval period after the establishment of a priory here in the twelfth century.

Twinham was a burh, one of a series of defended places at strategic points built by King Alfred to defend his kingdom against the Danes. Despite this strategic importance and command of a good harbour, Twinham does not seem to have been economically successful. It did not, for example, have a mint. The street plan of the burh is likely to have been a simple one – a single street along the top of the promontory – and this can be seen in today's street layout. The rivers and marshland to the south and east would have been an important part of the burh's defences, perhaps with banks and ditches across the northern part of the promontory.

Following the Norman Conquest, William Rufus gave the town to Ranulf Flambard, bishop of Durham, who demolished the Saxon church and began to build a new one. Bishop Flambard fell out of favour and was exiled, and the town and church passed to Richard de Redvers. The shell of the new church was incorporated into the Augustinian priory founded here around 1150 by Baldwin de Redvers, and building work continued. The nave was not completed until 1234, but has remained virtually unchanged to the present day. The priory exerted a strong influence on the economy of the town, which did not develop an independent trading life. Besides a small cloth industry and a little fishing, the fortunes of the town remained dependent upon the priory. At the dissolution most of the priory buildings were demolished, but the church became the parish church.

A motte and bailey castle, the motte a prominent feature in this photograph **100**, was built here around 1100 by Richard de Redvers. A stone keep was added to the castle around 1300.

Another surviving feature of the Norman castle is the great hall, the main accommodation block of the castle, known as The Constable's House. The castle was besieged and captured in 1148 but, although refortified, saw little action afterwards and had no real strategic importance; its main role was as a residence. Despite this, Parliament ordered the destruction of the castle in 1651.

100. Christchurch Priory and Castle
(Ministry of Defence/RAF)

101. Poole (Ministry of Defence/RAF)

Purbeck and Poole Harbour

101. Poole is situated on a peninsula which until the eighteenth century was more or less an island separated from the mainland by a boggy creek. Poole is not mentioned in the Domesday Book, being part of the manor of Canford Magna, which in 1086 was held by Edward of Salisbury. At that time, Poole seems to have been a fishing village or small port serving the manor, but grew rapidly. The rise of Poole in the thirteenth century coincided with the silting up of Wareham and the western end of Poole Harbour and the introduction of ships with deeper draughts. Poole served as a port for the import of building materials for Corfe Castle and the export of Purbeck stone.

The 1332 Lay Subsidy Roll entry for Poole reveals a small and relatively poor town, but in 1341 Poole was made a free borough, with burgesses taking all tolls. A record of an inquisition in 1341 lists imports to Poole. These include staves and poles, fish, hides, skins, wool, resin, and coal. As well as trade, the town was at this time renowned for piracy, to such an extent that in 1405 a joint French and Spanish force attacked Poole in revenge. In 1433 Poole replaced Melcombe Regis as the Port of the Staple, or the county's premier port. At the same time, a licence was granted to fortify the town, and the Town Gate may date from this time. Trade and fishing continued to dominate Poole's economy. During the Civil War Poole was the main Parliamentary garrison in Dorset. In the eighteenth century the town's wealth came largely from trade with Newfoundland, and it suffered accordingly when the trade collapsed in the early nineteenth century. The town's Great Quay and many private jetties along the waterfront were gradually swallowed up by reclamation, and development since the eighteenth century has greatly altered the town.

Some traces of Poole's medieval street layout survive, for example a triangular area around the guildhall has been identified as a possible medieval marketplace. The railway follows the line of the town dyke and the island on which the town once stood is now joined to the mainland by reclaimed land. Much of the old town was demolished as part of large-scale redevelopment in the 1960s and after.

Considerable evidence of late Iron Age and Roman occupation has been found at Hamworthy, across the channel from the town of Poole. A first-century military site here seems to have been a port supplying the great fort at Lake Farm, north of Poole. Later Hamworthy developed as an industrial settlement. Purbeck was the scene of much industrial activity during the late Iron Age and Roman period. The commonly used domestic pottery known as Black Burnished Ware was manufactured in the area, and utensils and ornaments fashioned from Kimmeridge shale were traded throughout Britain and exported to the continent. Salt-making was an important local industry in the Roman period. There is some evidence that local stone was quarried and traded relatively locally. Though the shale and pottery industries declined, the quarrying of Purbeck Stone revived and flourished in the medieval and post-medieval periods.

102. Wareham Town
(National Monuments
Record, 20 May
1992)

102. Wareham is situated on a long, narrow peninsula between the rivers Piddle and Frome. Finds indicate that there was a settlement here in the Iron Age and Roman periods, but the main period of development of the town in the form which we see today was in the Saxon and medieval periods. The town was a cross-Channel port in the eighth century, and according to the Anglo-Saxon Chronicle *Brihtric*, king of Wessex, was buried in Wareham in 802. This photograph shows clearly the massive earthen banks of the Saxon town walls, which have had a powerful influence on the way Wareham has developed. The present street plan, for example, is likely to date from this early period. In the left foreground is the site of Wareham Castle, built in the corner of the Saxon defences in the twelfth century. In 1762 a large part of the town was destroyed by fire, and many of the brick buildings in the town centre date from the subsequent rebuilding.

104. Duck decoy, Wareham St Martin (SW, 21 July 1995)

103. Wareham Quay and Wareham Lady St Mary (SW, 21 July 1995)

103. Wareham Quay is an ancient structure, repaired in 1745, and rebuilt in the nineteenth century. In this quarter of the town is a cluster of buildings which survived the catastrophic fire of 1762. Notable amongst them is the magnificent parish church of Wareham Lady St Mary, whose Saxon nave survived until 1841.

104. One of a pair of decoy ponds which are thought to have been constructed at Wareham St Martin in the early part of the eighteenth century since they appear on Taylor's 1765 map of Dorset. This pond is partly overgrown, but it is possible to see traces of the pipes or tunnels at the corners of the pond into which wildfowl were enticed.

105. Poole Harbour and Arne
(DCC)

105. Poole Harbour was an open landscape in the Neolithic period, gradually inundated by rises in sea-level. Though dredging of the channels will have removed some archaeological remains, it is generally felt that much remains to be discovered preserved beneath the harbour silts. There is considerable evidence of industrial and farming activity here in the late Iron Age and Roman periods. The sandy heathlands around the harbour were sparsely populated in medieval times. A new town, 'Newton', was founded on the southern edge of the harbour in Arne parish but failed to prosper.

106. Brownsea Castle (SW, 1995)

106. Brownsea Castle. The Victorian façade of Brownsea Castle conceals a Tudor fort, part of Henry VIII's chain of coastal defences. Early maps show Brownsea Castle as a square, single-storey building with a moat on three sides and on the fourth side an hexagonal gun platform commanding the entrance to Poole Harbour. The castle was built and maintained by the town of Poole. Though supposedly finished in 1547, the town accounts suggest that work continued sporadically for several years. In 1551, for example, 101 piles were set, perhaps to combat encroachment by the sea. Work was put in hand again in 1571 following complaints that the castle was ruinous. In 1764 the castle was acquired by Humphrey Sturt, who built it up into a four-storey tower with low wings on either side. It changed hands several times and was enlarged again in the nineteenth century. The castle was damaged severely by fire in 1892 and rebuilt in 1897.

107. Swanworth Quarry, Worth Matravers: the modern face of industry in Purbeck (SW)

108. Powerstock Castle
(National Monuments Record, 12 April 1983)

Castles

An early form of castle is the *motte and bailey* – an earth mound surrounded by an enclosure with a pallisade and with timber buildings. Many castles of this type were established by the Normans, built in great haste in the few years following the Conquest. Though these castles served as places of refuge, it seems their prime purpose at this time must have been to intimidate the local population, a tangible reminder of the strength and permanence of Norman domination. Other motte and bailey castles were thrown up in the turbulent years of Stephen's reign (1135–54). Documentary evidence is scarce, but many motte and bailey castles seem to have been occupied only briefly before being abandoned.

In the middle years of the twelfth century those at the most important locations were replaced by stone-built castles surrounded by massive ramparts. A typical feature of late twelfth and early thirteenth-century castles is a stone keep. By the early fourteenth century the cramped accommodation offered by keeps was generally abandoned, and expenditure concentrated on the construction of extensive and elaborate private apartments. Licences to crenellate were granted in large numbers in the fourteenth century as local magnates, wishing to add every possible embellishment, sought permission to top curtain walls and residential buildings with battlements. In more settled times under the Tudors castles fell out of fashion and were either converted or abandoned for elegant country houses. Some were refortified during the Civil War, only to be dismantled after the Parliamentarian victory.

108. Powerstock Castle. A motte and bailey castle on a promontory to the south-east of Powerstock village. The motte is defended on the north by the fall of the ground, and on the other sides by a ditch. The motte and bailey are likely to be eleventh or twelfth century in date. Powerstock was visited

109. Castle Hill, East Chelborough (SW, 21 August 1995)

frequently by King John. It has been suggested that the outer enclosure is older, perhaps even prehistoric, but there is as yet no archaeological evidence to confirm this. Medieval cultivation terraces, or strip lynchets, can be seen in the fields which swirl around the castle.

109. Castle Hill, East Chelborough. Two motte and bailey castles. The better preserved has an irregular bailey and a motte formed by steepening the natural scarp of the top of the hill. Traces of a narrow ditch can be seen in places around the motte. The earthworks have been much damaged by erosion and the northern side of the motte by quarrying in particular. The second castle, 150 metres to the east, is thought to be a siege castle. Both may be thirteenth century.

CORFE CASTLE

110. Corfe Castle and the Purbeck Ridge (Ministry of Defence/RAF)

110, 111. Corfe Castle stands on a steep, largely natural mound in a narrow gap in the Purbeck chalk ridge, commanding traffic into Purbeck and dominating the countryside and Poole Harbour.

The castle was built around 1080, and extended in the twelfth and thirteenth centuries with some later additions and alterations. Excavations have produced evidence of pre-Conquest buildings, and this may have been the site of a royal residence; it is known that King Edward the Martyr was assassinated at Corfe in 978. The castle was certainly a royal residence later, and played an important part as an administrative centre during the reign of King John.

During the Civil War the castle was in the possession of Sir John Bankes, Lord Chief Justice, and was held for the King from 1643 to 1646 by Lady Bankes. When the castle fell Parliament ordered its demolition by mining and explosion. The initial development of the town of Corfe Castle almost certainly depended on the presence of the castle, but the stone trade soon came to play an important part in its economy. Physically, the town has always been dominated by the castle, with the two main streets running away from the marketplace and the church at the castle gate.

*111. Corfe Castle
(SW, 21 July 1995)*

*112. Corfe Castle and The Rings
(SW, 21 July 1995)*

112. The earthwork in the right foreground, known as 'The Rings', was built during an earlier civil war – the Anarchy of the twelfth century, when Stephen and the Empress Matilda struggled for the throne. This rare example of an earthwork ring with adjoining bailey was probably constructed in 1139, when Corfe Castle was besieged by Stephen's supporters, and is thought to have been used as a defensible place from which attacks could be made.

113. Sherborne Old and New Castles
(SW, 28 July 1994)

113. Sherborne Old and New Castles face each other across an ornamental lake fed by the River Yeo. Sherborne New Castle was begun by Sir Walter Raleigh, and extended in the seventeenth, eighteenth and nineteenth centuries. The landscaped park is largely eighteenth century. The creation of Sherborne Lake began after Capability Brown had been consulted by the 6th Lord Digby in 1756. The town of Sherborne can be seen in the background.

114. Sherborne Old Castle
(SW, 28 July 1994)

114. Sherborne Old Castle was built by Roger, Bishop of Salisbury, between 1107 and 1135. The unusual layout, with the south-west tower one of several buildings around a central courtyard, dates from this earliest period of construction, and relatively few additions have been made. In 1592 the property was acquired by Sir Walter Raleigh, who began restoration but abandoned it in order to build a new house some 400 metres to the south. The castle fell into disrepair, but played a part in the Civil War and was besieged by Fairfax for sixteen days in 1645. On surrender the castle was partly demolished and rendered untenable.

115. Mohun Castle, South Perrott. This castle is a simple, moated enclosure. The surviving earthworks show that the moat once enclosed an area of about one third of an hectare, but is now dry and the northern part has been destroyed by an extension to the churchyard. In this photograph an apparent entrance in the south side of the moat and other enclosures to the south and east can be seen.

115. Mohun Castle
(National Monuments Record, 14 April 1977)

95

116. Eastbury, Tarrant Gunville
(SW, 20 July 1994)

Homes and Gardens

There are many fine country houses in Dorset. They range from country homes to magnificent houses set in extensive parks. Aerial photographs enable us to appreciate these houses in their setting, and to understand parkland designs.

116, 117, 118. Eastbury, Tarrant Gunville. Eastbury House was begun in 1718 by Sir John Vanbrugh for George Doddington, and largely demolished in 1775. In photograph **116** part of the seventeenth century formal gardens designed by Bridgeman can be seen as crop-marks. A long vista from the house at the western end of the gardens culminated at the eastern end in a terraced amphitheatre and a portico, called the Great Temple, visible in the picture.

The formal gardens at Eastbury were surrounded by a landscaped park. Both park and garden fell into disrepair and were altered considerably in later years. Particularly clear in photograph **117** are the remains of an avenue of tree-covered hillocks which were constructed as part of Bridgeman's design. Note the crop-marks in the foreground. Photographed only a few months later (**118**), the avenue of mounds can be seen as soil-marks in the recently-ploughed field.

117. (left) Eastbury tree mounds (SW, 20 July 1994)

118. (right) Eastbury tree mounds after ploughing (SW, 8 September 1994)

*119. Forde Abbey
(FR, 19 July 1990)*

119, 120. Forde Abbey, Thorncombe. The Cistercian abbey of Forde was founded as a daughter-house of Waverley in 1136, and moved to its present site in 1141. Parts of the original buildings, notably the Chapter-House, survive to the present day. Extensive building work was undertaken during the rule of the last abbot (Thomas Charde, 1521–39), when a new Abbot's Lodging was built. With the Dissolution, the Abbey passed into private hands.

In 1649 the property was bought by Edmund Prideax, Cromwell's Solicitor General, and a period of remodelling commenced. Little is known about how the park and gardens looked at this time, though paintings by Edward Prideax (1727) show formal gardens with avenues and a Long Pond, which survive in today's layout.

In the 1930s Geoffrey Roper began the restoration and redevelopment of the gardens. The main South Avenue was replanted with black walnut and lime, and new developments included an arboretum.

In July 1989 (**120**) the layout of a past garden design was captured as parch-marks in the present lawns.

121. Bridehead, Littlebredy. Bridehead is set in an early nineteenth-century landscaped park. The landscaping scheme included the re-design of the estate village of Littlebredy and a lake, formed in the 1830s by the damming of the River Bride (in the foreground). Parts of the house date from the sixteenth century, but it was largely remodelled by Peter Frederick Robinson in 1831–3.

120. Forde Abbey lawns
(Devon County Council, July 1989)

121. Bridehead
(FR, April 1995)

122. Lulworth Castle and Park
(FR, 17 August 1994)

122. Lulworth Castle and Park. Brick-built with facings of Purbeck and Portland stone, Lulworth Castle is a simple, severe building of three storeys above a basement with four-storey towers at each corner. Building work began in the late sixteenth/early seventeenth century. Work on the exterior was complete by about 1609, and few additions have been made since. The castle, which was gutted by fire in 1929, has recently been conserved. This photograph shows the castle in its parkland setting. In the 1790s the village of East Lulworth was moved to allow landscaping, and this photograph shows earthworks of what may be the original site of the village, in the parched grassland beyond the castle.

123. Wolfeton. The circular towers of the gatehouse give Wolfeton House something of the appearance of a castle, but the gatehouse was built around 1500 and is unlikely to have been intended to fulfil any defensive role. The south range of the house itself was built a little later in the mid-sixteenth century.

124. Athelhampton House was built in 1493 for Sir William Martyn. The house was enlarged in the sixteenth century and remodelled in the early seventeenth century, towards the end of the nineteenth century, and again 1920–21. Francis Inigo Thomas produced designs for the formal gardens around 1891. Further restoration and development of both house and gardens has been undertaken since 1957. Rows of pyramidal yews make a particularly eye-catching feature of the present gardens.

123. Wolfeton House
(FR, 4 November 1996)

124. Athelhampton
(FR, 25 May 1997)

125. Roman Roads at Badbury Rings
(National Monuments Record, 21 April 1976)

Communications

125. Roman roads near Badbury Rings. Rather than this being a junction as we understand it, these crop-marks show how one road crosses another. It seems that these roads were not in use at the same time. Roman roads usually took the form of a built-up causeway, or *agger*, with ditches at either side.

126. Roman road at Oakley Down. The course of the Roman road from Old Sarum to Badbury Rings is preserved as an earthwork and in the line of later field boundaries.

127. Melbury Beacon. Before the advent of modern communications technology, large areas could be alerted to danger by the lighting of hill-top beacons. The most commonly feared threat was invasion. A network of beacons was established in the medieval period, and maintained in the Tudor period and during the Napoleonic wars in particular. It seems unlikely that the slight, almost perfectly circular, earthwork we see here played any part in the use of the hill as a beacon, since beacons were usually built of stone. A more probable explanation of the earthwork is that it is the remains of a relatively modern plantation enclosure.

126. Roman Road at Oakley Down
(SW, 8 September 1994)

127. Melbury Beacon
(SW, 21 July 1995)

128. Poundbury
(National Monuments Record, 2 February 1971)

128. Poundbury. When the railway line between Weymouth and Bristol was built in 1855 it was proposed to blast a cutting through the Iron Age hill-fort at Poundbury on the edge of Dorchester. Public outcry stimulated much interest in archaeological matters in the county and led eventually to the foundation of the Dorset Natural History & Antiquarian Field Club (now the Dorset Natural History & Archaeological Society). This picture shows clearly how the railway company was obliged to bow to public opinion and tunnel beneath the hill-fort. Note the industrial estates under construction when this photograph was taken in 1971.

*129. Railway line at Maiden Newton
(DCC)*

*130. Tarrant Rushton Airfield, completed in May 1943, was the
main base from which the 6th Airborne Division departed for
Normandy in the early hours of D-Day (DCC)*

131. Dorchester by-pass (National Monuments Record, 28 August 1987)

131. This photograph shows the western part of the Dorchester by-pass under construction in 1987. A number of archaeological sites were discovered during preliminary work by Wessex Archaeology commissioned by the County Council, and subsequently excavated before the road was built. Part of a Neolithic causewayed enclosure was excavated at Flagstones, next to Thomas Hardy's house, Max Gate (right foreground).

The Passage of Time

The study of aerial photographs enables us to monitor the condition of archaeological features over time.

132, 133. Two views of Badbury Rings, a complex multi-vallate hill-fort enclosing just under 7 hectares, situated on a prominent chalk knoll overlooking the Stour Valley.

133. Badbury Rings
(National Monuments Record, 20 July 1994)

132. Badbury Rings
(National Monuments Record)

134. Buzbury Rings
(National Monuments Record, 8 May 1980)

134, 135. Buzbury Rings, Tarrant Keyneston. An enclosed rural settlement, which was first built in the Iron Age and continued in use into the Romano-British period. Finds from this site include Iron Age and Romano-British pottery, animal bone, and wattle and daub (presumably from the walls of huts). The inner enclosure seems to have been the main area of settlement. The monument is crossed by a road and partly occupied by a golf course.

135. Buzbury Rings
(National Monuments Record, 8 September 1994)

136. Oakley Down barrow cemetery
(John Boyden, February 1969)

137. Oakley Down barrow cemetery
(SW, 8 September 1994)

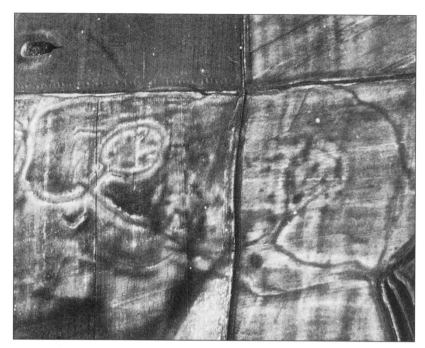

138. Iron Age enclosures, Gussage All Saints (John Boyden, March 1971)

139. Iron Age enclosures, Gussage All Saints (FR, April 1991)

140. The effects of coastal erosion on the Flowers Barrow hill-fort are all too evident (FR, August 1994)

Where to See the Photographs

The Dorset Sites & Monuments Record
Environmental Services Directorate
Dorset County Council
County Hall
Dorchester
DT1 1XJ   Tel. 01305 224921

The Dorset Record Office
Bridport Road
Dorchester
DT1 1 RP   Tel. 01305 250550

Dorset County Museum
High West Street
Dorchester
DT1 1XA   Tel. 01305 262735

Cambridge University Committee for Aerial Photography
Mond Building
Free School Lane
Cambridge
CB2 3RF   Tel. 01223 334575

Royal Commission on the Historical Monuments of England
National Monuments Record
Kemble Drive
Swindon
SN2 2GZ   Tel. 01793 414600

Further Reading

Aerial Photography

Riley, D., *Aerial Archaeology in Britain*, Shire Publications (1982)

Whimster, R., *The Emerging Past: Air Photography and the Buried Landscape*, RCHME (1989)

Wilson, D.R., *Air Photo Interpretation for Archaeologists*, (1982)

Wilson, D. R. (ed.), *Aerial Reconnaissance for Archaeology*, Council for British Archaeology (1975)

Cranborne Chase

Barrett, J., Bradley, R., and Hall, M. (ed.), *Papers on the Prehistory of Cranborne Chase* (Oxford, 1991)

Bowden, M., *Pitt Rivers* (Cambridge, 1991)

Parker Pearson, M., *Bronze Age Britain* (1996)

Monuments

Cunliffe, B, Wessex to AD 1000 (1993)

Wainwright, G.J., *Mount Pleasant, Dorset: Excavations 1970–1971*, Society of Antiquaries Research Report no.37 (1979)

Woodward, P.J., *The South Dorset Ridgeway. Survey and Excavations 1977–84*, Dorset Natural History and Archaeological Society Monograph no.8 (1991)

Boundaries

Bowen, H.C., *The Archaeology of Bokerley Dyke*, RCHME (1990)

Hill-forts

Cunliffe, B., *Iron Age Britain* (1995)

Fitzpatrick, A., and Morris, E. (ed.), *The Iron Age in Wessex: Recent Work*, Wessex Archaeology (1994)

Sharples, N., *Maiden Castle* (1991)

Wheeler, M., *Maiden Castle*, Society of Antiquaries Research Report no.12 (1943)

Woodward, A., *Shrines and Sacrifice* (1992)

Towns and Villages

Darby, H.C., *Domesday England* (Cambridge, 1977)

Draper, J., and Chaplin, C., *Dorchester Excavations. Volume 1*, Dorset Natural History and Archaeological Society Monograph no.2 (1982)

Good, R., *The Lost Villages of Dorset* (Wimborne, 1979)

Hinton, D., *Archaeology, Economy and Society* (1990)

Loyn, H.R., *Anglo-Saxon England and the Norman Conquest* (1986)

Myres, J.N.L., *The English Settlement* (Oxford, 1989)

Penn, K.J., *Historic Towns in Dorset*, Dorset Natural History and Archaeological Society Monograph no.1 (1980)

Platt, C., *Medieval England* (1978)

Rowley, T., and Wood, J., *Deserted Villages*, Shire Publications (1982)

Schofield, J., and Vince, A., *Medieval Towns* (Leicester, 1994)

Smith, R.J.C., *Excavations at County Hall, Dorchester, Dorset, 1988*, Wessex Archaeology Report no.4 (1993)

Welch, M., *Anglo-Saxon England*, Batsford, 1992

Churches

Curl, J.S., *Victorian Churches* (1995)

Rodwell, W., *Church Archaeology* (1989)

Fields and Farms

Bettey, J., *Rural Life in Wessex 1500–1900* (Gloucester, 1987)

Kerr, B., *Bound to the Soil* (1968)

Rackham, O., *The History of the Countryside* (1986)

Taylor, C., *Fields in the English Landscape* (1975)

Monasteries

Victoria County History, *Dorset*, ii (1912)

Portland and the Fleet
Saunders, A., *Channel Defences* (1997)

The Coast
Jarvis, K.S., *Excavations in Christchurch 1969–1980*, Dorset Natural History and Archaeological Society Monograph no.5 (1983)

Purbeck and Poole Harbour
Sunter, N., and Woodward, P., *Romano-British Industries in Purbeck*, Dorset Natural History and Archaeological Society Monograph no.6 (1987)

Castles
Brown, R.A., *English Medieval Castles* (1954)
McNeill, T., Castles (1992)

Homes and Gardens
Bettey, J.H., *Estates in the English Countryside* (1993)

Brown, A.E. (ed.), *Garden Archaeology*, Council for British Archaeology (1991)
Taigel, A., and Williamson, T., *Parks and Gardens* (1993)

Communications
Good, R., *The Old Roads of Dorset* (1940)
Smith, R.J.C., et al., *Excavations Along the Route of the Dorchester By-pass, Dorset, 1986–8*, Wessex Archaeology Report no.11 (1997)

The passage of time
Darvill, T., *Ancient Monuments in the Countryside* (1987)
Groube, L.M., and Bowen, M.C.B., *The Archaeology of Rural Dorset: Past, Present and Future*, Dorset Natural History and Archaeological Society Monograph no.4 (1982)

List of Subscribers

Abbey House, Abbotsbury
Mrs J. Ackerman, Dorchester, Dorset
Graham and Susan Adams, Dorchester, Dorset
M.J. Addison, Harmans Cross, Dorset
Mrs Janet Adlam-Hill, Dorchester, Dorset
Marian Albery, Overcombe, Dorset
Dr Michael J. Allen, Codford, Wiltshire
William J. Allenby, Kenilworth, Warks
Mrs Brenda Ambrose, Stourton Caundle, Dorset
Richard Ames, New Barnet, Herts
Cecil Amor, Bridport, Dorset
James M. Anderson, Dorchester, Dorset
Ian Andrews, Poole, Dorset
Olive and Peter Arnold, Stoke Abbott, Beaminster, Dorset
John Ash, Ferndown, Dorset
David Ashford, Dorchester, Dorset
Professor Mick Aston, Winscombe, Somerset
Julie I. Athill, West Parley, Dorset
Donald M. Bacon, Weymouth, Dorset
Alan G. Bailey, Wimborne, Dorset
Heather L. Bailey, Weston-super-mare, Somerset
John Bailey, Long Bredy, Dorset
P.E. Bailey, Beaminster, Dorset
Allan Baker, Wareham, Dorset
G.C. Ball, Upton, Dorset
Mr G.D. Ball, Oakhill, Somerset
John Barker, Wool, Dorset

Ken and Nicki Barker, Bookham, Dorset
Dr Margaret Barker, Dorchester, Dorset
Mrs L. C. Barrie, Sherborne, Dorset
Keith W. Barter, Bournemouth, Dorset
Stanley C. Batcheler, Child Okeford, Blandford Forum, Dorset
H.G.A. Bates, Wareham, Dorset
Mrs Audrey Beall, Merley, Dorset
Dave and Sue Beardsmore, Stalbridge, Dorset
Mrs Margaret Beetham, Dorchester, Dorset
Angela Bell, Langton Matravers, Dorset
Mary Bell, Langton Matravers, Dorset
Peter Bell, Kingston, Corfe Castle, Dorset
Donald Bennett, Weymouth, Dorset
Mrs H. Bennett, Gillingham, Dorset
Tony and Ann Bennett, Stoborough, Dorset
Wayne Bennett, Toller Whelme, Dorset
Mr P.J. Beresford, Okeford Fitzpaine, Dorset
Dr Robert H. Bewley, RCHME, Ashton Keynes, Wiltshire
Mary Birkill, Dorchester, Dorset
Hilton G. Blandford Ieng, Amraes, Windsor, Berks
Anthony Bletsoe, West Parley, Dorset
Keith Blockley West Moors, Ferndown, Dorset
A. Blofield and C. Hawkey, Christchurch, Dorset

Ann and Phil Bloor, Sherborne, Dorset
C. Bond, Doncaster, S. Yorks
Mr Will Bond, Wareham, Dorset
Mike Bone, Keynsham, Bristol
Carole A. Boseley, St Albans, Herts
Brian Boston, Charmouth, Dorset
Dr H.J.M. Bowen, Blandford, Dorset
E.A. Bowers, Ringwood, Hants.
Kitchie Box, Halstock, Somerset
Diana Bradley, London W12
S. Bratcher, Winterborne Whitechurch, Dorset
Bob Breach, East Melbury, Dorset
Mr P. H. Brentnall, Poole, Dorset
Anthony H. Briggs, Fifehead Neville
Roger H. Briggs, St Ives, Ringwood, Hants
E. F. and M. Brooks, Bournemouth, Dorset
Leslie B. Broughton, Bridport, Dorset
David Broughton, Weel
Leslie Broughton, Wembworthy
Ann and Leslie Brown, Child Okeford, Dorset
Canon Bernard Brown, Dorchester, Dorset
Betty Brown, Bournemouth, Dorset
Mrs J.E. Brown, Tarrant Keyneston, Blandford Forum, Dorset
Jill and Robert Brown, Milton Keynes
John F. Brown, Weymouth, Dorset
Michael C. Brown, Poole, Dorset
Simon Brown, Wimborne, Dorset

Mrs E.L. Bubb, Weybridge, Surrey
Paul Budge, Christchurch, Dorset
Mrs Ruth Buley, Dorchester, Dorset
Violet A. Burch, Shaftesbury, Dorset
Valerie I. Burd, Gillingham, Dorset
Richard F. Burden, Dorchester, Dorset
Verity Burgess, Chelmsford, Essex
Brian and Margaret Burt, Wimborne,
   Dorset
John Bush, Winterborne Zelston, Dorset
Michael Bushell and Kay, New Zealand
Mrs M. R. Cadel, Wootton Fitpaine,
   Bridport, Dorset
Diane Calcott, Lowestoft, Suffolk
Mr J. Cameron, Winterborne
   Whitechurch, Dorset
Anne Cargill, Swanage, Dorset
Dorothy Carr, Wareham, Dorset
Mrs S. Caunt, Buckingham, Bucks.
Tim Chambers, Milborne St Andrew,
   Blandford, Dorset
Miss C.A. Chantler, Reading, Berkshire
Mr I.C. Chantler, Huddersfield
Mr and Mrs P.D. Chantler, Bridport,
   Dorset
A. John Chapman, Churchdown,
   Gloucester
Cynthia Childs, Dorchester, Dorset
John Christmas, Dorchester, Dorset
Christine Clarke, Burton Bradstock, Dorset
Dennis R. Clark, Broadmayne
Mary Clark, Dorchester, Dorset
Michael Clarke ,Weymouth, Dorset
Dr Wendy A. Clark, Bournemouth
   West, Dorset
Peter C. Clarke, Budmouth T.C.
Richard J. Clarke, Sturminster Newton,
   Dorset

R.J. Clarke, Bristol
Anne and Geoffrey Collins, Dorchester,
   Dorset
Fred Cook, Broadmayne, Dorset
Peter Cook, Surbiton, Surrey
Bill Coomer, Sturminster Marshall,
   Dorset
Babs Cooper, Weymouth, Dorset
Colin Cope, M.A., White Mill, Dorset
Mrs Corbett, Weymouth, Dorset
Sally Courtenay, Sturminster Newton,
   Dorset
Donald E. Cox, Weymouth, Dorset
Keith L. Cox, Weymouth, Dorset
P. J. Crabbe, Macclesfield, Cheshire
Richard Crocker, Weymouth, Dorset
B.J. Croydon, Weymouth, Dorset
Cecil N. Cullingford, Broadstone,
   Dorset
Jenny and Simon Dalton, Corscombe,
   Dorset
Jean A. Davies, Weymouth, Dorset
Lin Davies, Portland, Dorset
Serena E. Davies, Weymouth, Dorset
W.R. Davies, Wimborne, Dorset
Mike Davis, Bridport, Dorset
Muriel E. Davis, Pimperne, Dorset
R.J. Davis ,Poole, Dorset
Mrs Sheila Davis, Gillingham, Dorset
C. Deaves, Cheselbourne, Dorset
Mrs J.P. Dibdin, Bridport, Dorset
Christopher Dickson, Glanvilles
   Wootton
John and Eileen Dickson, Dorchester,
   Dorset
Marian J. Dixon, Yarm, N. Yorks
Nick Dixon, Westbury, Wiltshire
Roger Dixon, Gillingham, Dorset

Penny A. Dolan, Abbotsbury
P. Donnelly Preston, Dorset
Mr A.W. Downs, Boscrege, Cornwall
Dread at the Controls, Lytchett
   Matravers, Dorset
G.W.J. Drew, Oxford, Oxon
Linda Duffy, Weymouth, Dorset
Cathryn S. Dukes, Bournemouth, Dorset
Vivienne C. Dunstan, Weymouth,
   Dorset
John R.T. Dyer, Dorchester, Dorset
East Devon Heritage Trust, Wimborne,
   Dorset
J.M. Eayrs, Alderley Edge, Cheshire
Gerald M. Edwards, Swanage, Dorset
Neil Edwards, Wyke Regis, Weymouth,
   Dorset
Martin and Ruth Elliott, Manchester
Sara Elliot, Weymouth, Dorset
Sheila I. Elliott, Christchurch, Dorset
Brian Ellis, Poole, Dorset
Kenneth Rainforth Emmett, Caernarfon,
   Gwynedd
Mr A. English, Organford, Poole,
   Dorset
D.B. English, Esq., Parkstone, Dorset
Robert M. Evetts, Ufford, Suffolk
Richard Ewan, Sherborne, Dorset
Mr J.O. Fairfax, Wimborne, Dorset
Phyllis E. Farthing, Dorchester, Dorset
R. Featherstone, RCHME
Christopher G. Finch, Redbourn, Herts.
J.M. and A.P. Flather, Wimborne,
   Dorset
Brenda Flint, Wimborne, Dorset
Mrs L. Forti, London
Mrs R.V. Fowler, Yeovil, Somerset
Michael J. Fox, Crowthorne, Berks

Dr Peter Fox, Puncknowle, Dorchester, Dorset

Mr David Fritzlan, Sturminster Newton, Dorset

G. and H. Frost, Buckland Newton, Dorset

David J. Fry, Okeford Fitzpaine, Dorset

Roy Fursey, Netherbury, Dorset

John Gadd, Fontmell Magna, Dorset

Miss Betty Galton, Dorchester, Dorset

Christopher D. Gardner, Warwickshire

Ghislaine Garvey, Walton-on-Thames, Surrey

Chris Gee, Hitchin, Herts

Geraldine Gee, Hitchin, Herts

June P. Gent, Southbourne, Hants

Mrs A. M. Gerrish, Wokingham, Berks

J.H.P. Gibb, Sherborne, Dorset

Ruby Gibbs, Balls Cross, Petworth, West Sussex

Ian Gibson, Dorchester, Dorset

(Dr) James Gibson, Cerne Abbas, Dorchester, Dorset

Mr and Mrs B.C. Gittos, Yeovil, Somerset

Rex Goddard, Alton Pancras, Dorset

Kevin Goldstein-Jackson, Poole, Dorset

Mrs A. J. Gooch Broadstone, Dorset

P. Goodall, Lytchett Matravers, Dorset

Alban Graham, Frampton, Dorset

Dr Leslie W. Graham, Corfe Mullen, Dorset

Lt. Col. G.E. Gray, Wimborne, Dorset

Lee K. Greenhow, Sittingbourne, Kent

Harry Grenville ,Frampton, Dorset

Mr R. J. Griffiths, Upholland, Lancs

Dr M. C. Grundy, Poole, Dorset

Hilda Gudge, Bridport, Dorset

W.G. Gundry, Dorchester, Dorset

Stephen Guy, Curry Rivel, Somerset

Clare and Tim Haggett, Bicton, W.A. and Arne

Peter and Brenda Haggett, Chew Magna, Dorset

Mrs Eveline W. Hallett, Wimborne, Dorset

T. Hallett, Weymouth, Dorset

John Hamshaw Thomas

Christopher Hamshaw Thomas, Sturminster Newton, Dorset

Mrs K. A. Hanna, Barton-on-Sea, Hants

Anthony M. Hansford, Portland, Dorset

Ms C. Hardy, Portland, Dorset

Brian J. Harper, Weymouth, Dorset

Joan M. Harris, St Leonards-on-Sea, East Sussex

Dr Gerald Hart, Dorchester, Dorset

Frank Harwood, Whitstable, Kent

Joan Hathaway, Enfield, Middlesex

Andrrew Hawkes, Poole, Dorset

Brian Hawkins, Lydlinch, Dorset

J.W. Hawkins, Godmanstone, Dorset

Anthony Head, Tokyo

Terry and Margaret Hearing, Martinstown, Dorset

Trevor W. Hearl (Poole)

Mrs J. Hearn, Frome St Quintin, Dorset

Dr Alan R. Hedges, U.S.A.

Gerald J. Hedges, Poole, Dorset

Dr John M. Hedges, Mappowder, Sturminster Newton, Dorset

Mr Mark Helfer, Knitson, Dorset

Michael Henderson, Seaborough, Dorset

Heather Hersey, Blandford, Dorset

I. Hewitt Poole, Dorset

Keith H. Heybourne, Child Okeford, Dorset

Tim and Vanessa Heywood, Bournemouth, Dorset

Donald Hibberd, Alderholt

Betty Hicks, Stenhousemuir

Simon Hicks, Bristol

Peter Higginson, Winterborne Zelston, Dorset

David A. Highmore, Maidenhead, Berks.

Shelagh M. Hill, Sherborne, Dorset

David J.B. Hindley, Corbridge, Northumberland

David A. Hinton, Southampton

Mrs P. Hoare, Weymouth, Dorset

Erica M. Hobbs, Melbury Osmond, Dorset

Maria W. Hobley, Dorchester, Dorset

Mary E. Hobley, Thorncombe

Geraldine Hobson, Hazelbury Bryan, Dorset

M. Hodges, Blandford Forum, Dorset

Michael Holt-Chasteauneuf, Henfield, West Sussex

Mr Patrick Horne, Bradford, Ontario

Anthea Hughes, E. Sheen

Harold C. Hughes, Bournemouth, Dorset

Alan John Humphries, Wimborne-St-Giles, Dorset

Sarah Humphries, Broadoak, Dorset

Lyn Hunt, Parkstone, Poole, Dorset

Joan and Ken Isaac, Welwyn, Herts.

S. Jackson, Swanage, Dorset

Brian James, Bournemouth, Dorset

Vera H. Janaway, Bridport, Dorset

Stuart and Sue Jane, Charmouth

Simon and Carol Janes, Cranborne, Dorset
Peter Jarvis, Wyke, Gillingham, Dorset
Geoffrey Jay, Wroxall, Isle of Wight
Dr S.L. Jeffcoate, Dorking, Surrey
Mr D.A. Jeffers, Dorchester, Dorset
John R. Jeffries, South Perrott, Beaminster, Dorset
Robert Jenvey, Portland, Dorset
Mr B. J. Johnson, Wareham, Dorset
Daphne Johnstone, Bristol
Bob and Angela Jones, Charmouth
Brian C. Jones, R.A.W.C., Cranborne, Dorset
Celia and Peter Jones, Fremantle, W.A.
Mrs Maureen Keats, Dorchester, Dorset
Jake Keen Wimborne, Dorset
Gareth Keller, Shepperton, Middx
Pamela Keller, Bridport, Dorset
David R. Kelley, Caterham, Surrey
Jane Kellock, Dorchester, Dorset
Mrs A. Kemp, Sutton Poyntz, Dorset
Mr A.M. Kemp, London
Geoffrey R. Key, Kenilworth, Warks.
Sara E. Key, Kenilworth, Warks.
Frank Kibblewhite, Sherborne, Dorset
Ann and Michael King, Wareham, Dorset
Mr Leslie Kitzerow, Sherborne, Dorset
John A. Lake, West Moors, Ferndown, Dorset
R.G. Lane, Weymouth, Dorset
Desiree Lang, Arne, Dorset
Jean Langdon, Burton Bradstock, Dorset
Mr C. Langston, Bridport, Dorset
P. Laurie, Abbotsbury, Dorset
Dr and Mrs M. J. Le Bas Blandford Forum, Dorset

Elizabeth Leedam, Puddletown, Dorset
Mrs E. Leonard, Ringwood, Hants
Mr Paul William Levey, Rochford, Essex
George W. Lewis, Corfe Mullen, Dorset
Mrs Lidsey, Gillingham, Dorset
Hugh Lindsay, Dorchester, Dorset
Mrs. J. Lister, Theberton, Suffolk
Barbara Livingstone, Poole, Dorset
David W. Lloyd, Harlow, Essex
Tim Loansby, Dorchester, Dorset
Dr Peter Lock, York
Janet and Leslie Long, Taunton, Somerset
Ceri Long, Beaminster, Dorset
Lorna Low, Dorchester, Dorset
Mrs D.A. Lucas, Wimborne, Dorset
Richard C. Maby, East Melbury, Shaftesbury, Dorset
James and Muriel MacGregor, Wimborne Minster, Dorset
Mrs J.H. Mackey, Portland, Dorset
Melanie Mackie, Glasgow
Mrs A. M. Marston, Great Missenden, Bucks
Pamela R. Martin, Beccles
Mr C.J.B. and Mrs M.M. Martin, Morton Heath, Dochester, Dorset
Mrs C.O. Martin ,Weymouth, Dorset
Dennis G. Martin, Poole, Dorset
Mason Family, Bournemouth, Dorset
David Masters, High Storrs, Sheffield
G. McConnell ,Askerswell
Maurice McPherson, Sevenoaks, Kent
David Mead ,Wyke Regis, Weymouth, Dorset
John D. Medd Christchurch, Dorset
Bob and Enid Mercer, Child Okeford, Dorset

Derek and Joan Mills, Cranborne, Dorset
Howard Mills, Little Bredy, Dorset
Simon and Sally Mills, Cranborne, Dorset
C.N. Milner, Weymouth, Dorset
John Milner, Horton, Dorset
Priscilla I.M. Minay, Dunfermline
S.M. Minhinnick ,Dorchester, Dorset
Mrs Ann M. Monk, Bournemouth, Dorset
Clifford N. Monk, Bournemouth, Dorset
Mrs Gillian H. Moore, Stourton Caundle, Dorset
Suzy and Simon Morgan, Pontypridd, South Wales
Ann and Aubrey Morle,y Sherborne, Dorset
Stuart Morris ,Portland, Dorset
Esther M. Morris-Jones, Burton-on-Trent, Staffs.
Jo Mosen, Swanage, Dorset
Mr K.S.D. Mossman, Verwood, Dorset
P.F. Moule, Sherborne, Dorset
Jeffrey A.C. Mowlam, Dorchester, Dorset
Joss Mullinger, Maidenhead, Berks
Gemma Murley, Bridport, Dorset
Elinor C. Murphy, Shaftesbury, Dorset
Francis J. Murphy, Blandford St. Mary, Dorset
Bryn Nash, Burton
J. Nash, Winterborne Kingston, Dorset
Anne Nelson ,Weymouth, Dorset
Paul Newell, Luton, Bedfordshire
Dorothy and Paul Newsome, Bournemouth, Dorset
Ken and Fay Nicklen, Verwood, Dorset

Richard and Joy Nicklen, Winton, Dorset
Mrs D.W.B. Nimmo, Blandford, Dorset
Ms V.L. Norman, Stafford, Staffs
Leonard J. Norris, Lytchett Matravers, Dorset
Pamela C. Norris, Lytchett Matravers, Dorset
Mrs E.J. North, Ealing, London W13
Jenny Oliver, Poole, Dorset
Miss A.M. Orr, RRC, and Miss M.A. Taggart, BA, Lyme Regis, Dorset
Mr and Mrs Hugh Orr, Toronto, Canada
Michael and Valerie Oxley, Poole, Dorset
Colin E. Pack, Burbage, Leics
Judi and Gordon Page, Ferndown, Dorset
John Patrick, Wareham, Dorset
Denis Paxman, Cumbria
John J. Pearson, Dorchester, Dorset
R.N.R. Peers, Beaminster, Dorset
Miss Linda Penfold, Harrow, Middx
John and Josephine Pentney, Taunton, Somerset
Shirley Percival, Lytchett Matravers, Dorset
Reg Perry, Portland, Dorset
Cllr Jonathan Pethen, Poole, Dorset
Charles Pettit, Banbury, Oxon
John and Barbara Phillips, Dewlish, Dorset
Royston A. Phillips, Willenhall, W. Mids
Barbara Pinder, Doncaster, S. Yorks
Robert G. Pinder, Doncaster, South Yorkshire
Gerald H.D. Pitman, Sherborne, Dorset

Mona Pitman, Bridgwater, Somerset
Roy Pitman, Shepton Mallet, Somerset
H.J. Platt, Dorchester, Dorset
Francis J. Plowden, London
Mrs M.I. Porteous, Shaftesbury, Dorset
George Powell, Weymouth, Dorset
Miss Sheila Powell, Sherborne, Dorset
Tony Poyntz-Wright, Taunton, Somerset
B. J. Precey, Bishops Stortford, Herts
Andrew Price, Sutton Poyntz, Weymouth, Dorset
Mrs K. Priest, Dorchester, Dorset
Mrs L.P. Puley, Bridport, Dorset
W.G. Putnam, Dorchester, Dorset
Hilmary Quarmby, Melbury Osmond
Mrs Janet Quinn, Sherborne, Dorset
Nancy M. Raison Pylle, Shepton Mallet, Somerset
D.L. Randle
Nicky and Caleb Ranson, Macclesfield, Cheshire
RCHME, Swindon, Wiltshire
Mrs J. Read, Dorchester, Dorset
Norman Read, Bournemouth, Dorset
P.G. Redgment, Portland, Dorset
N.M. Redwood, Ferndown, Dorset
Dennis and Sheila Ricketts, Poole, Dorset
Eric A. Roberts, Swanage, Dorset
Phil and Marion Roberts, West Lulworth, Dorset
Darren Robinson, Bristol
Giles J. Romanes, Dorchester, Dorset
Rosemary Rooke, Cranborne, Dorset
Karen A. Rumsey, Piddletrenthide, Dorset
David P. Russell, Dorchester, Dorset
Roy Russell, Poole, Dorset

B. Samuels and M. Lucas, Christchurch, Dorset
Peter Saunders, Branksome Park, Poole, Dorset
R.J. Saville, Langton Matravers, Swanage, Dorset
Mrs O.C. Schartau, Corscombe, Dorset
Mrs J.A. Scott, Whipsnade, Beds.
Dennis R. Seaward, Chetnole, Sherborne, Dorset
Kevin Senior, Linslade, Beds.
Robert Shave, Plush, Dorset
Julian Shepherd, Nether Compton, Dorset
The Library, Sherborne School, Sherborne, Dorset
R.G. Sherwood, Bournemouth, Dorset
The Revd S.N. Shrimpton, Grantham, Lincs
R.M. Silberrad, Sherborne, Dorset
O.S.L. Simon, Sturminster Newton, Dorset
Tim Smallman, Weymouth, Dorset
Dorothea F. Smith, Yeovil, Somerset
Frank and Lynette Smith, Poole, Dorset
Ian F. Smith, Brampton, Ontario, Canada
Margaret R. Smith, Worcestershire
Peter R. Smith, Timsbury, Bath
B.W. Sneddon, Weymouth, Dorset
Dr Marja Soots, Willowdale, Ontario
C. Spencer, Bournemouth University, Poole, Dorset
J. Stacey, Cranborne, Dorset
David Stafford, Bournemouth, Dorset
Allan Stainer, Hedgerley, Bucks.
Ken Standing, Poole, Dorset
Sheila E. Staples, Birdsmoorgate, Dorset

Wendy Stevens, Weymouth, Dorset
Mrs E. Stevenson, Godalming, Surrey
Eric St C. Stobart, Studland
Mrs J. Sullivan, Portland, Dorset
Jo and Paul Summerfield, Bridport, Dorset
Dr H.A.H. Summers, Walsall, West Midlands
D.R. Symonds, Dorchester, Dorset
Arthur and Ann Tait, London and Arne
Brian and Margaret Tait, Dorchester, Dorset
Gordon and Jane Tait, Eaglescliffe
Janice M. Tait, Swanage, Dorset
Mike Tait, London
Alan and Patricia Tate, Corfe Mullen, Wimborne, Dorset
Douglas Taylor, Wimborne Minster, Dorset
Joan Taylor, Bridport, Dorset
Mr G.W. Tegerdine, Gillingham, Dorset
Ernest H. Terry, Gillingham, Dorset
Hilary Thomas, Sherborne, Dorset
J. Thomas, Harrow, Middx
M. F. Tighe, Mere, Wiltshire
Christine Tilley, Bournemouth, Dorset
W.R.A. Toop, Salisbury, Wiltshire
J.P.L. Tory, Bryanston, Dorset
Brenda J. Toulouse, Poole, Dorset
J.M. Tulloch, Wareham, Dorset
Clare J. Turnbull, London
Mr B. Turner, Farnborough, Hants
Peter John Upshall, Manswood, Wimborne, Dorset
Mrs P.H. Vale, Cerne Abbas, Dorset
Van Millingen Family, Newlandrig
Mrs L. Vaughan, New Milton, Hants

Michael Wade, Sandbanks, Poole, Dorset
Peter F. Waldron, Wareham, Dorset
Mrs Doreen M. Walker (Cheselbourne), now Waresley, Herts
P.A. Walker, Shaftesbury, Dorset
Carolyn M. Waller, Puncknowle, Dorset
Dorothy Wallis, Shaftesbury, Dorset
John Wallis, Bovington, Dorset
Sarah Wallis, Ringstead
Mrs D.M. Walters, Burton St. Marnhull, Sturminster Newton, Dorset
Major E.J. Warren, MBE, RM, Dorchester, Dorset
Mr J. Waterworth, Higher Ansty, Dorchester, Dorset
Marion Watson, Wimborne, Dorset
Robert M. Watt, Moorside
Dr Janet Waymark, Petts Wood, Kent
Janet Weatherley, Bridport, Dorset
Audrie and Don Webber, Highcliffe
Sonia Webber, Beaminster, Dorset
Col. and Mrs T. Weeks, Brecon
Mrs C.R. Wells, West Chiltington, West Sussex
Norman Welsford, Beaminster, Dorset
Robin T. Westmacott, Burnley, Lancs
Derek Whatmoor, Owermoigne, Dorset
Richard Whatmoor, Nottinghill
David J. White, Swanage, Dorset
Jeanette Whittaker, Talbot Village, Poole, Dorset
Les Whittaker, Spetisbury, Dorset
Margaret Whittam, London
Phil Wicks, Brentford, Middx
K.P. Wightman, Glastonbury, Somerset
T.R. Wightman, Sherborne, Dorset

Richard Wilding, Twickenham, Middlesex
Norman G. Wilkins, Ryme Intrinseca, Dorset
Clive and Pat Willetts, Winterbourne Abbas, Dorset
H. Mary Wills, Corfe Castle, Dorset
Mr A.F. Wilmott, Weymouth, Dorset
Mr and Mrs Michael Wing, Wheathamstead
Miss Stephanie Wing, Arkley, Herts
D.V. Winks, Sherborne, Dorset
A.J. and R. Wise, Wareham, Dorset
Mrs P.M. Wise, Eastleigh, Hants.
Alan and Christine Wiseman, Blandford Forum, Dorset
G.R. Wiseman, Dorchester, Dorset
Canon Eric Woods, Sherborne Abbey, Dorset
N. Woods, Poole, Dorset
Wally and Chris Woodward, Weymouth, Dorset
John Worth, King's Stag, Dorset
Lesley and Mik Wray, Milborne Port, Dorset
John P. Wreford, Bath
Mr and Mrs J.W.P. Yates, Chichester, West Sussex
R.A. Yates, Dorchester, Dorset
Anthony E. Yeatman, Wimborne, Dorset
Yeovil College Archaeology Library, Yeovil, Somerset
Graham F. Young, Weymouth, Dorset
Mary Yoward, Emsworth, Hants